OUTDOOR HOME
IDEA BOOK

OUTDOOR HOME
IDEA BOOK

The Taunton Press

The Taunton Press
Inspiration for hands-on living®

The Taunton Press, Inc., 63 South Main Street, PO Box 5506,
Newtown, CT 06470-5506
e-mail: tp@taunton.com

ILLUSTRATORS: Christine Erickson and Martha Garstang Hill
COVER PHOTOGRAPHERS: Front cover: (top row, left to right) ©Brian Vanden Brink,
©Lee Anne White, ©Deidra Walpole, ©Brian Vanden Brink; (bottom row, left to
right) ©Tim Street-Porter, ©Linda Svendsen, ©Brian Vanden Brink, ©Dency Kane.
Back cover: (top photo) ©Tria Giovan; (bottom row, left to right) ©Chipper Hatter,
©The Taunton Press, Inc., ©Jerry Pavia, ©Tim Street-Porter.

Library of Congress Cataloging-in-Publication Data

Outdoor home idea book.
    p. cm.
  ISBN-13: 978-1-56158-861-9
  ISBN-10: 1-56158-861-X
 1. Outdoor living spaces.
  NA8300.O98 2006
  728'.93--dc22
                              2005035511

Printed in Singapore
10 9 8 7 6 5 4 3 2 1

Contents

Contents (continued)

Exterior Appearances

A house is a complicated piece of architecture. Not only is it three-dimensional, but it's also made up of a host of major components, from the foundation to the roof. The front of a house is called the façade, and anything and everything that can be seen from the street—the siding, roof, windows, front door, and supporting features like shutters—plays a role in how your home is perceived by others. Understanding how these components work together is the key to creating a home with true curb appeal.

Making the most of your home's exterior appearance can be a simple matter of changing the paint color, altering the siding, or adding a new window or front door. On the other hand, the front of your house may be a candidate for serious rethinking: It may require a comprehensive makeover, such as expanding the front porch to create an outdoor room, and change the entire look of the façade.

No matter how you improve your home, however, it's important to create a unified, overall appearance for your home's "face" so it looks its very best.

◄ STUCCO DOESN'T have to be white or pastel in color. On this sage-green stucco house, trim possibilities range from dark forest greens to rich brick red. The owners chose a soft brown that is only slightly darker than the ground color.

Playing Up Your Best Features

ALL HOUSES HAVE A SENSE of style. These days, however, architectural elements are combined with so much abandon that it can be hard to pin down exactly what style your home is. For example, a Ranch house could easily have Colonial features like a fanlight and window shutters while a Cape might have a front porch trimmed with Victorian millwork.

No matter. Whether you consider your home traditional or contemporary, it's more important that the house project a sense of flair that's pleasing to you. While it can be helpful to add details or paint colors that are characteristic of an identifiable style (such as white with black shutters on a 1920s Colonial), allow yourself the freedom to be creative. That means choosing materials, colors, and textures that both complement the look of your house and express your personal style. Maybe that white Colonial would look even better with a lavender front door. It's all a matter of working with what you've got—and doing what you like.

◄ MORE TRADITIONAL than contemporary, this impressive home mixes a variety of bold textures and fanciful architectural features, like a three-sided tower and an eyebrow window in the slate roof. Windows grouped in threes help unify the exuberant façade.

▲ THIS HOUSE PROJECTS a sense of style that's neither old nor new but a little bit of both. While the lines are crisp and contemporary, the house is finished with shingles used three different ways—a technique borrowed from late 19th-century homes.

◄ THE EXTERIOR OF A HOUSE doesn't have to be fancy to have curb appeal. The charm of this simple home lies in a single unifying color. The steps are clean and uncluttered, and vertical battens on the siding provide some relief.

MAKING A STATEMENT

▲ SMALL TOUCHES TO A HOUSE can add a lot of charm. These wishbone-shaped brackets underneath a deep eave demonstrate just that. The brackets not only frame the corner window, but also subtly point to the flower box just underneath it.

▲ STRONG ARCHITECTURAL FEATURES like a tin roof and natural-finish shingles and siding make this home a standout. A large part of its appeal comes from the careful positioning of the windows—two underneath the peaked gable in the bump-out and two framing the peak in the porch roof.

▲ THIS STUCCO HOUSE gains tremendous visual impact from bold, propped-out Bermuda shutters that double as sun guards. While traditional shutters emphasize the shape and positioning of windows, these emphasize the flowing lines of the roof, making the house seem larger.

▲ A BROAD VERANDA with a low-pitched roof makes a bold statement and makes this one-story house seem much larger. Deep porches are an excellent way to increase your home's curb appeal. In effect, they add an extra room to the house, which is especially ideal in warm locales.

◄ HOMES RIGHT ON A ROAD often turn a blind face outward. But that doesn't mean your home can't be attractive. This homeowner finished the front with narrow battens and repeated them overhead in exposed rafter tails. Latticework with lush greenery adds a cool color and softens the exterior.

Architectural Elements

WHEN YOU LOOK AT THE exterior of your home, what do you see? The largest, most obvious elements are the siding or cladding, the roof, and the windows. If you focus your energies on making sure these components look good both individually and together, you will greatly enhance your home's appearance.

It's easy to take the siding for granted, whether it's brick, wood, stone, metal, or stucco. But don't make that mistake! You can always change the color of the cladding and the trim around windows and doors or choose different textures (for example, rough stucco versus smooth). The roof is equally important: It can easily make up half of what the eye sees on a home's exterior. As for windows, it's important that they are well sized and positioned; a poorly placed or ill-sized window can make the entire face of a house look off-kilter.

◀ THE MAJOR ELEMENTS—roofing, siding, and windows—all work together to give this cottage an inviting, unified appearance. The roof, windows, and covered entry porch are all outlined with painted green trim—a trick that helps to pull the façade of a house together.

◀ TUCKED AWAY UNDER AN EAVE, a window with shutters gets a lift from a bracketed window box filled with flowers. The lavender supports do their part to create unity on the home's façade: They match the decorative brackets on a slight recess at the second-story level.

▲ THE STEEPLY PITCHED ROOF on this house dominates it in terms of style. Adding some charm and relief, however, are the diamond-paned windows and the peaked entry porch. Without these two important features, the roof would have been too much of an overpowering presence.

◀ A CONTEMPORARY DESIGN can look as though it has always been part of the landscape. Traditional building shapes like a sloping gabled roof and a shed porch reinforce the sense of past times, as do the unfinished shingles, a staple of early American homes.

SIDING AND CLADDING MATERIALS

▲ NOT ALL BRICK IS FLAT RED, as this home with its pinkish hues demonstrates. Manufacturers today offer brick in a wide range of colors and textures, with different blends available to suit any style of home, from traditional to the boldest contemporaries.

▶ A CLASSIC SIDING TREATMENT for early American homes is wood siding. Called clapboards, these are long, narrow boards installed horizontally across the face of the house. The boards are painted and overlap so that water will run off of them.

▲ TRADITIONAL IN HOT-WEATHER CLIMATES like the Southwest, stucco is an increasingly popular finish material for new homes today. Its smooth, subtle texture can suit a minimalist contemporary or serve as a backdrop for styles with a lot of decorative detail, like Neo-Spanish Colonial. Like wood, it can be painted any color.

▲ NATURALLY FINISHED WOOD is an attractive siding material for a contemporary home. The earthy color of the wood marries well with other natural materials, like stone, and helps tie the entire house to the surrounding landscape.

Choosing Cladding

UPGRADING THE SIDING ON your home is one way to improve its appearance. The most traditional choice is horizontal lap wood siding in cedar, redwood, or white pine. (Occasionally, wood siding is installed vertically and finished with battens, narrow strips that conceal the seams.) Alternatives include wood composites; these man-made boards are less expensive than real wood siding.

Other traditional cladding materials include shingles, which can be painted, stained, or left natural, and brick. Brick is more expensive than wood, but it never rots or needs painting.

Vinyl and aluminum, the least-expensive siding choices, are frequently installed as original siding on new houses today, often in a durable factory finish in the color of your choice. Although either material will last practically forever, the color fades and needs to be repainted after about 10 years. Both materials tend to show dirt more easily than wood, too.

If you prefer a romantic, Old World appearance, stucco and natural or synthetic stone are good choices but tend to be more expensive than other siding options.

▲ RICHLY TEXTURED BRICK STEPS create a pleasing contrast for a stucco house tinted a rosy pink. Two bump-outs on either side of the front door help to frame the entry; the walkway centered on the door reinforces the sense of balance.

◄ SMALL DETAILS, Like a lattice that conceals the exterior crawl space on this shingled house, are important finishing touches that keep the overall appearance of a house neat and clean. Paint a finishing piece like this in a related or contrasting color.

◄ RED IS A GREAT COLOR for siding. It looks good (and very different) whether it's paired with light or dark trim. It's also easy to match to a broad range of colors, especially those in the green family.

▲ A LOG HOME in a natural finish offers plenty of rough-hewn charm. Infill panels made of sapling-sized sticks add extra texture under a bay window, while crisp green paint on the trim gives the façade a little polish.

Siding Colors

JUST ABOUT ANY COLOR under the sun can work as a primary ground color on the exterior of a home. That said, some materials lend themselves to certain color palettes. Stucco, for example, looks best in a range of earth colors, from whites and pastels to greens and browns. Brick varies naturally depending on the type of clay in the mix, from light pinks and tans to deep reds and browns. While wood siding can be painted, it can also be stained or left natural, as can shingles, which weather to an attractive silver-gray if left untreated.

In addition to white, red and green are the ground colors that give the most latitude in picking a complementary trim color. Blues, on the other hand, are notoriously difficult to match.

THE ROOF

▲ THE SUPPORTS that hold up a roof are called rafters. Exposing the ends of the rafters is a wonderful way to add interest to the area under the roof. These rafter tails have been shaped with a saw to resemble the heads of horses.

▲ IT'S POSSIBLE TO ENLIVEN A ROOF without replacing the shingles or painting the eaves. This shingled cottage gets a burst of color from a climbing wisteria, which cascades over the edge of the roof from crest to gutter.

◄ PROVIDED IT'S KEPT PAINTED to avoid rusting, a standing seam metal roof can be an attractive and exceptionally long-lived roof. Versatile enough for most styles of homes, the base material is steel, copper, or aluminum. The standing seams are created with a crimping machine.

Roofing Materials

YEARS AGO, ASPHALT SHINGLES **were a foregone conclusion as the roofing material of choice on American homes. Although they're still popular, today's asphalt shingles come in a host of variations. Some have slightly varied overlap patterns to make them look more "architectural" and others have shadow lines to make them look like clay tiles. Still others are textured to resemble hand-split cedar shakes.**

Other traditional roofing options include barrel-vaulted clay tiles and thick, substantial slate tiles. You can find good value in look-alikes made of concrete or metal, though, which resemble the higher-priced traditional choices.

While most roofing materials are available in earth tones, the color possibilities may surprise you, ranging from almost black to red and orange, plus green and yellow.

Concrete

Clay

Metal

Slate

▲ ROOFING MATERIALS are surprisingly diverse these days. In addition to the ubiquitous asphalt shingle, there are concrete shingles that resemble asphalt and metal tiles that look like clay, as well as traditional materials like barrel-vaulted clay tiles and slate shingles.

WINDOWS

▲ WINDOWS THAT CRANK OPEN from the bottom are called jalousie windows. Arranged in a vertical bank of six on a contemporary house, these windows let in plenty of air but not rain. The angle also repeats the slant of the metal roof.

▲ A TRIPLE WINDOW IS A VERY OLD, very stylish combination. This triple window over an entry not only adds interest to the house, but also echoes the arrangement of sidelights around the front door. The lack of grillwork (or muntins) on the lower panes reinforces the home's Arts and Crafts style.

◄ RATHER THAN THINK of windows as single units, imagine the possibilities when they're paired up in twos, threes, or fours. Although these windows are small and narrow, together they create a large, picturesque span that lets in a lot of bright light.

Window Types

THERE ARE SEVERAL BASIC WINDOW TYPES that make good style choices for a majority of homes. The first is the colonial-style window. These tall, well-proportioned windows line up in rows horizontally and vertically, and are evenly spaced around the front door. Each window is double hung, meaning there are two individual sashes. Each sash is divided into individual panes by a grid. Colonial windows usually have at least six panes per sash, top and bottom.

A second window type is the Arts and Crafts window. These windows can also be double hung, but only the top sash is divided into individual panes (usually with four or six panes of glass). Arts and Crafts windows are often grouped in rows of three or more.

Contemporary windows tend to be large pieces of plate glass. While they can be any size, it's still important to align them in rows.

Colonial

Arts and Crafts

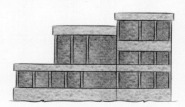

Contemporary

Shutter Styles

S HUTTERS DRESS UP a window. The traditional shutter comes in pairs, with one shutter placed on either side of a window. Shutters can be louvered (vented slats), paneled (solid with some relief), or board and batten (a rustic style). It's also possible to personalize shutters by cutting whimsical shapes—diamonds, acorns, or quarter moons, for example—into the bottom panel.

Whereas louvered or paneled shutters are usually fixed in place, Bermuda shutters pop open like an awning over a window. Bermuda shutters can be louvered or constructed of vertical boards. In addition to supplying protection from hot sun in warm climates, they also protect windows during storms when closed.

▲ NOT ALL SHUTTERS swing open at the side. In warm climates or seaside locations, Bermuda shutters traditionally open from bottom to top to create shade and let in breezes. They lock down to protect the house during bad weather or for winterization.

◄ A PLAIN WINDOW on a simple house can take on charm with the addition of shutters and a well-filled flower box. Choosing flower colors that complement or match the color of the house will intensify the impact of the display.

▼ SIDE SHUTTERS are a throwback to Colonial times, when many windows didn't have glass in them. Today's shutters, however, are mostly decorative and are fixed in place. Even so, they can create a lot of impact on traditional homes, which can look bare and naked without them.

► VICTORIAN HOUSES offer both the charm of gingerbread millwork and large, sunny windows—traits that make the style a popular one to copy today. Pairing up windows in twos and threes goes a long way in opening and flooding the interior of a home with warm, natural light.

◄ WINDOWS ARE USED lavishly on this English country-inspired home to bring in light and add charm. The tall vertical windows fit nicely into the scheme that uses half-timbering on the top story, while the attractive details called quoins accent the smaller windows.

DETAILS

▲ PLAY UP THE ROMANTIC possibilities of your house with details. Here, projecting rafters exaggerate the line of the roof. This technique—a favorite used on Arts and Crafts houses—also creates a good spot for a hanging light fixture.

▲ DON'T OVERLOOK the possibilities for decoration on large pieces of house trim like gutters and downspouts. Here, a decorative plate with a floral pattern adds a bit of flair without adding substantial cost.

▲ THE EXPOSED RIVER ROCK on the chimney of this cottage is a romantic, whimsical detail typical of Arts and Crafts homes that would be easy to incorporate into the design for a chimney on a newer house.

▲ DECKS, PORCHES, and even latticework covering a raised basement can benefit from a unified approach to design. The top section of the porch railings repeats the square grid of the latticework, while arched trusses soften the impact of all the straight lines.

◄ STONE IS A traditional foundation material, but these rounded boulders are just for show—an inventive way to cover a crawl space. Lattice, low-growing shrubs, and tinted concrete are a few other ways to conceal or even beautify an unsightly, exposed foundation.

2

The Entry

Nothing goes further toward creating good feelings for a home than an attractive front door. But there's much more to an inviting entry passage than a mere portal. For one thing, the entry must be a strong focal point, so visitors know where to enter. That's the reason so many doors are placed front and center on a house.

At the same time, the entry marks a division between public and private space. A successful entry offers a pleasing face to passersby yet maintains interior privacy for you and your family. For that reason, it's important to consider other elements beyond the door— the door frame, sidelights, stoops and steps, covered entries, and larger porches—when evaluating your entry. Large or deep entry porches, for example, not only protect the front door from inclement weather, but they can darken interior spaces. If your home has one of these, you may want to add glass in or around your door to brighten things up.

Details are especially important around the entry, too. Hardware, lighting, plants, and additional items like screen doors can all have a tremendous impact on an entry's overall appearance.

◄ PAINT THE CEILING on a deep porch a light color to help reflect more light into the house. Light blue is traditionally found on porch ceilings, in part because it mimics the sky but also because the shade helps to reduce glare.

The Front Door

THE DOOR TO YOUR HOME is probably the first thing any guest or visitor sees. Even if the door isn't attractive on its own merits, there are many ways to enhance that important first impression. Positioning is key: Most doors should be centered between other large architectural elements, like windows, columns, or a covered entry porch, to create a sense of importance. If the door is on the side of the house, it helps to have strong elements that point to it—side panels or an entry porch, for instance.

The door itself should be distinctive. If the style isn't particularly impressive, paint the door an attractive color. It's perfectly fine to use bold hues like red, black, or even lavender on the front door, provided you don't go overboard with color elsewhere on the front of the house. Key the style of the door to the overall style of your home (traditional, contemporary, or rustic). If need be, you can also simply replace the door!

▲ SOME DOOR DESIGNS are especially friendly and welcoming. This paneled wood door features a bank of window panes at the top that resembles a traditional sash window. Supporting details include a horizontal "sill" underneath the panes, plus block details.

◀ A FRONT DOOR recessed into the side of an arched opening might be hard to spot. For that reason, the owner has added a pretty, arched-shaped trellis covered with vines to alert visitors to its presence.

▲ THIS ENTRY DOOR in warm wood is highly successful because so much of what leads to it is attractive. A covered entry and a set of railings are both painted a clean, crisp white. Landscaping touches, including a climbing vine over the porch lantern and potted plants in full bloom soften the architecture and add color and texture.

◄ ALTHOUGH THE DOOR is rather plain, other features on this house make it a desirable focal point. The entry is flanked on either side by matching windows with shutters and window boxes, and the door is centered under a peaked gable, painted a soft green.

TRADITIONAL ENTRY DOORS

▲ FORMAL DOORS are often symmetrically balanced. To achieve this kind of look, use elements in threes and fives. This Arts and Crafts–style entry has five panels and three leaded-glass windows. Another way to create symmetry is to place light fixtures or potted plants on either side of the door.

◄ A PANELED DOOR in a beautiful and long-lived wood like mahogany gives a house a sense of solidity and formality. To increase the door's presence, this one is trimmed with an arched surround that includes sidelights and a spiderweb-patterned fanlight over the entire entry.

◄ THIS COLONIAL HOME has two entries: the formal one in the center, and a side entrance facing the driveway that is probably used more often. Both entries share similar traditional characteristics, like formal trim work and side lights.

Sidelights

ONE WAY TO BRIGHTEN a doorway and give it more importance is to add sidelights, vertical panels of glass that run on each side of a door frame. Sidelights (a light is the architectural term for a pane of glass) help to illuminate a front room or entry hall without sacrificing privacy, especially if the glass is patterned or colored, as with leaded glass. They also tend to add balance and proportion to an entry, so they're often used when the front door is a side entry rather than a center one.

Sidelights can be paired with an arched fanlight or a horizontal glass panel over the door, called a transom. The width of the transom can match the width of the sidelights, or it can be narrower or wider—whatever makes the entry look most balanced.

ART GLASS LETS IN LIGHT but maintains privacy by keeping out prying eyes. Here, leaded-glass sidelights in a flowering-tree pattern enliven an Arts and Crafts entry door. The transom is about half the width of the sidelights, which creates a sense of harmony and balance.

Door Types

R AISED PANEL DOORS ARE PROBABLY the most familiar door style. The door gets its name from the pairs of vertical panels that seem to "float" between the flat cross and side pieces that hold them in place. There are usually four or six panels to a door.

Arched doors are often composed of a rounded raised panel at the top and a rectangular panel at the bottom. The arched shape lends itself well to paired doors.

A cottage-style door has two or three narrow vertical panels at the bottom and one or more panes of glass at the top. Suitable for many types of houses, cottage doors lend themselves to inserts of leaded glass and additions like transoms and sidelights.

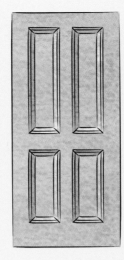
Raised panel

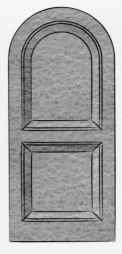
Arched

Cottage style

► IF YOUR FRONT door is strongly one style, embellish it with other characteristics of that style. This Victorian entry is enriched by an abundance of Victorian features, including a leaded glass front door, an elaborate, horseshoe-arched screen, and a cascade of flowering plants. Amidst purple hues, the light brown door is an unmistakable standout.

▼ THIS TRADITIONALLY STYLED entry door is not only attractive but wheelchair accessible, too. The key to accessibility is to eliminate any steps on the approach and to minimize any height variations between the exterior decking, the interior floor, and the threshold. The door opening should also be at least 36 in. wide.

▲ THE IDEA OF a broad horizontal beam framing an entryway comes from classical Greek architecture. Although this side entry door is already well-proportioned and balanced by sidelights, the temple-like shape adds an extra measure of formality.

▶ CLASSICAL FORMS LIKE ARCHES are also traditional for front doors. The arch over this entry is repeated in the Spanish-style arch in the roofline. A lantern hung high over the door reinforces the sense of balance.

▲ TRADITIONAL DOESN'T ALWAYS mean formal. This door, recessed under a porch, is especially welcoming because the glass panes repeat the two-over-two pattern of the sash windows. A hand-chiseled granite column adds an element of surprise.

► WHEN THE DOOR and siding material are similar in tone or color, use bold or bright trim to increase the visibility of the entry. The blue-gray trim surrounding the doorway makes this traditional Arts and Crafts door stand out.

◀ A FANLIGHT is a glass panel over the door in the form of a shallow arch. Fanlights, like columns, are another way of adding formality to an entry. This one has the extra twist of appearing under the covered entry porch rather than directly over the door.

Door Color

DOORS CAN BE PAINTED, stained, or sealed to let the natural beauty of the wood shine through. Almost any color can be used, since you want the door to call attention to itself.

White, black, and red have always been popular choices, but for the venturesome, choose a bold color that complements your cladding or siding, including greens, yellows, blues, or even startling colors like purple or lavender.

If you'd rather have a rich or bold color on your siding instead of the door, paint the door the same color as the trim. Use a glossy paint, preferably enamel. Early American doors are often treated to multiple coats of high-gloss enamel paint, with a sanding in between each layer, until the finish is so smooth and shiny that you can almost see your reflection in it.

▲ BECAUSE RED ADDS WARMTH to the façade of a home and goes so well with many colors, it is an excellent choice for a front door. This example stands out clearly against the white siding and is a natural complement for the blue shutters.

CONTEMPORARY AND RUSTIC ENTRY DOORS

▲ ALTHOUGH THE STYLE of this door is contemporary, it does many of the traditional things we expect a door to do: It lets light in through its grid of rectangular glass panes, yet is difficult to see through. To ensure total privacy within the foyer of your home, use colored, leaded, or frosted glass.

▲ WOOD ADDS WARMTH to any house, especially when the door is in the form of naturally finished vertical planks with exposed knots. A rectangular panel of glass adds a touch of delicacy to the rough lines of the door and lets in some light.

▲ DETAILS ON A casually rustic entry door reinforce the traditional style of this Spanish adobe house. The door is recessed under a shallow stucco arch, which provides much-needed shade in warm climates. The glass panel at the top of the door lets some light stream into the foyer.

▲ THE ENTRY ON THIS LOG HOME uses the traditional form of a raised-panel door but with playful materials—tree bark on the panels, stick dividers in the arched fanlight, and a bone door handle. The mix of natural textures adds interest to what could have been an otherwise simple wood door.

◄ OVERSIZED AND completely flat, this entry door echoes the use of rectangular panels of glass elsewhere in this mid-century Modern house. The door is not completely plain, however. The entry hardware is substantial and a shiny metal kick panel, which protects the bottom of the door, adds a bit of flash.

▼ THE EARLIEST AMERICAN doors were crude affairs, made of rough-hewn boards held together by cross pieces, often without nails. A vertical glass panel slightly off-center in this plank door gives it a more contemporary appearance.

▲ COMBINING DIFFERENT TEXTURES can be a good way to make an entry eye-catching. A door framed by peeled logs seems perfectly in keeping with a house trimmed with rough-cut siding, columns made of stone, and a pebbled entry porch. Interesting details include a grate over a square peep-hole.

▲ EVEN AN ENTRYWAY with plenty of concrete can incorporate the formal ideas of balance and symmetry. Here, concrete walls enfold the courtyard, and concrete pillars and glass sidelights frame the entry door. A jazzy metal pergola arched at an angle overhead puts a contemporary spin on things.

◄ A FORMAL DOOR can seem rustic with the right finish treatment. Although this entry is composed of a pair of arched paneled doors, the streaky green paint color (created by layering different shades of paint for effect) gives it an aged, well-worn appearance.

The Right Accents

SMALL DETAILS can make the difference between a doorway that shines and one that simply falls flat. Once you've carefully chosen a new front door or livened up your old door with a fresh coat of paint, give just as much consideration to essentials like entry hardware, the lighting over or beside the door, and any other accents that fall within the immediate vicinity, from porch furniture and flower pots to door numbers and the mailbox.

The one door accessory that's most often overlooked is the storm/screen door (a door frame with interchangeable screen and glass panels). If you have a metal storm door with an initial on it from the family who lived in your home 40 years ago, it's probably time to replace it with a new one more in keeping with the style of the house. Screen doors can either be metal or wood, and they lend themselves to a variety of styles.

▲ ENRICHMENTS CAN BE ADDED to doors where you least expect them. This paneled mahogany door in a warm, natural finish becomes something out of the ordinary with the addition of carvings of local ground covers and wildflowers. Although this door is custom made, you may be able to get something similar from a high-end door maker.

2648

◄ FOR THE SAKE of delivery people and new visitors, most house numbers should be at least 4 in. high so that they are easy to read from the street. Many stylish options abound, from traditional numbers like these to ceramic and metal versions in a variety of styles, from Art Deco to Arts and Crafts.

◄ THE RIGHT LIGHT FIXTURE creates a safe and inviting approach to any home. Choose outdoor fixtures that complement the particular style of your home—black iron lantern styles for Early American homes, hammered metal and art glass for Arts and Crafts homes, and sleek metal for modern houses, for example.

▲ SELECTIVELY PLACED VINES or shrubs like this climbing rose can reward you with an entry that is particularly inviting. A vine-shaded arbor is an attractive solution for entries that get full sun but lack a porch. Here, a cozy seat, an almost transparent screen door, and a lantern sconce enhance the sense of welcome.

SCREEN DOORS

► A SCREEN DOOR can be painted to match the trim on the main door or, if it will be taken down in the winter, painted in an alternate color. A striking color, like the dark green used here, makes the door stand out.

► COUNTRY HOUSES and farmhouses practically beg for a screen door. This example with a T-shaped bottom is simple, yet sturdy enough to stand up to plenty of traffic. It's also painted the same color as the trim elsewhere on the house, so it blends in.

Screen Door Styles

IF YOU LIKE THE LOOK of your front door and simply want the option of bringing in light during the winter and fresh breezes in summer, choose an all-purpose combination screen/storm door with a large open panel and no trim. (The screen and the glass panels are interchangeable, usually popping easily out of the frame.)

For something a little more traditional but still versatile, opt for the Colonial style, which looks appropriate on many types of homes.

The simple intersecting lines of the Arts and Crafts–style door would suit many types of early 20th century homes, or Neo-Arts and Crafts homes built more recently.

The same holds for Victorian and Neo-Victorian homes, which can benefit from a little gingerbread trim on the screen door frame.

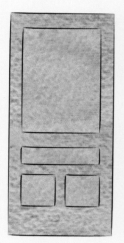
All purpose

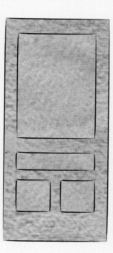
Colonial

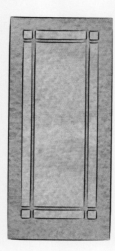
Arts and Crafts

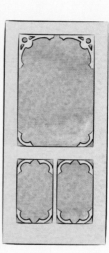
Victorian

◀ A HOUSE WITH VICTORIAN ELEMENTS will benefit from a screen door with a bit of gingerbread—usually tucked into the corners of the frame or around the center divider. This door is painted a dark color that contrasts pleasantly with the white siding on the house.

▶ A SCREEN DOOR can add a little style—or a lot—to a front door. This version includes a picket fence-like kick panel at the bottom that echoes the shape and spacing of the nearby porch railings. Such similar details help to tie the overall entry together.

DOOR HARDWARE

▶ VICTORIAN DOOR SETS are known for their elaborate, flowing patterns. A vintage set can really set off an entry, and it's possible to find a complete set, from doorknobs to strike plates, from architectural salvage dealers. Or shop for a good-quality reproduction online or at a local home store.

▲ NOT ALL DOOR HANDLES are found at the local hardware store. Since most visitors are likely to notice the doorknob and handle on an entry, this is a good place to add an exceptional detail found at an antique or salvage store, like this unusual cast-metal dragon.

◀ SINCE MANY DOORS get worn and dirty around the doorknob, a large entry plate (a piece called an escutcheon) can add extra protection. If the escutcheon is copper, brass, or bronze, the plate may acquire the added benefit of a handsome patina.

▶ DOOR KNOCKERS are functional, but they can also make attractive door accents. A knocker doesn't have to match the entry hardware precisely—choose one made of the same metal or in a related style, or go for broke with a novelty piece in an interesting shape, like a dolphin, cluster of grapes, or palm tree.

▲ THIS MEDIEVAL-LOOKING DOOR gains a lot of style points from a pair of elaborate strap hinges. Although every door has hinges, these are largely for show. House numbers located directly beneath the lighting fixture ensure this house can be easily found morning, noon, or night.

▲ STRAP HINGES ARE A STRIKING and inexpensive way to dress up a door because they don't have to be functional. The hinges can either match or contrast with the door pulls. The strap hinges here are a key decorative element for this entry.

◄ DECORATIVE GRILLWORK is another form of hardware for the front door. While this example reflects the California Mission style of this 1920s home, it's adaptable to other types of doors. The grillwork can be kept locked when the door is open, providing ventilation and adding extra security.

◄ STYLE DETAILS on certain types of houses should be matched right down to the door hardware. Arts and Crafts homes are especially well known for their use of hammered copper and details like the square cutouts on this door plate.

IN THE DETAILS

Mailboxes

A MAILBOX is another important entry detail that can be easily personalized. While sturdy and serviceable mailboxes are available at the local home store, you can also cast a wider net and get something unique.

Look for antique or reproduction mailboxes from architectural salvage dealers and specialty stores, or use an unusual but stout container. If you have a deep, covered porch, for example, employ a sturdy basket for mail deliveries—just be sure to mount it securely. If you can find a mailbox that's made of brass, bronze, or copper, the metal will age and perhaps even gain an attractive patina.

▲ THIS VINTAGE MAILBOX is made out of black metal. The openwork owl decoration on the front serves a practical purpose, enabling the owner to see at a glance whether or not the day's mail has arrived.

▲ A LETTER SLOT is an attractive way to receive mail. The disadvantage is that the mail will fall through the slot onto your hall floor. To keep things tidy, install a basket or an open box under the slot indoors to catch magazines and letters.

LIGHTING

▲ AN UNUSUALLY ELEGANT rust-brown lantern mounted high over a door makes a striking accent light against a wall of light-colored stucco. Overhead illumination can be just as effective as light thrown off by fixtures located on either side of the door—it's simply a matter of personal taste.

▲ EXTERIOR SCONCE LIGHTS for entry doors can be mounted shallow to the wall or project dramatically, like this Arts and Crafts example. A projecting sconce is likely to throw more light, but take care to install it high enough that you won't bump your head.

▲ SCONCES—light fixtures that attach to a wall rather than a ceiling—are a good way to illuminate an entry, especially when they are used in pairs. Position fixtures where they will cast light on steps and the front door lock so you're able to enter your home safely.

▲ SOMETIMES THE MOST EFFECTIVE exterior lighting comes from within. The openwork porches on this shingle-style contemporary home allow lighting on exterior walls and under porch eaves to bounce outward, making the entire house a warm and welcoming presence.

◄ EXTERIOR LIGHTING doesn't have to be fancy to be effective. A simple metal pendant light installed close under the roof eave lights up this rustic doorstep and helps illuminate the nearby stone patio. Interior lights just inside the porch add extra ambiance.

◄ WHILE A WALL SCONCE IS useful for shedding a little light around an entry or passageway, consider the decorative possibilities offered by lanterns like this one. The cut-metal overlay of tree branches will cast interesting shadows against a wall or porch ceiling.

▲ FOR A RUSTIC LOOK that sheds plenty of light over a front door, consider a radial-wave lamp. Shielded by a flared metal shade and with the bulb protected by a cage, these industrial-strength lights stand up to outdoor use.

▲ LANTERNS DATE BACK to times when lanterns were carried by hand and then hung up outside a door to shed light. They are a good choice for traditional homes like this farmhouse.

◄ THE LIGHTING SCHEME on this home is as eclectic as the façade materials. Although three types of fixtures are used, they're far enough away from each other to make their own statement yet complement the exterior of the home.

► IF THE APPROACH to your entry climbs a flight of stairs, add small "wash" lights just above foot level every step or two. Visitors will easily be able to see the way up the stairs without light shining in their eyes.

FINISHING TOUCHES

▲ ▶ HOUSE NUMBERS are an inexpensive way to add real flair to a front door. Attractive ones are available in a variety of metals and finishes for just a few dollars apiece. Coordinate them to other elements on your home, such as the front doorknob or a door knocker.

◄ THINK OF A RAIN CHAIN as a cross between a decorative downspout and a wind chime. A rain chain breaks the fall of the water from your roof, guiding the water downward. The sound is similar to a bubbling fountain or flowing brook.

▲ IF YOU LIVE IN AN AREA that gets plenty of rainfall, consider adding a rain chain to channel water from your roof to a splash-way or basin. Usually made of copper, rain chains can be shaped from linked chains, loops, inverted bells, or flower shapes.

▲ ALMOST ANY ELEMENT on your house can be decorative if you have enough imagination. These whimsical elephants made by a Vancouver copper-smith may not be to everyone's taste, but they are functional as well as artistic.

▲ ▼ A DOWNSPOUT can be a work of art in the right hands. Since a material like copper has to be cut and shaped to channel rainwater, it lends itself to decorative treatments like this thirsty fish.

▲ LITTLE DETAILS make a big difference around the front door. Even an element as small as a door buzzer can add a pinch of punch. Home stores and online suppliers offer dozens of styles, from a traditional fleur-de-lis to a contemporary bull's-eye.

▲ A DOOR KNOCKER not only makes a satisfying thunk when guests come calling but it also can be a signature statement for your door. Traditional door knockers include hefty loops that you grasp in one hand. The knocker either taps directly against the door or against a dedicated plate.

Landings and Porches

▲ IF SPACE PERMITS, a landing should have a bench or, at the very least, a small chair. This deck is just wide enough for a cozy bench with pillows and an old metal dairy sign as a backdrop. A potted evergreen and a wind chime make this an inviting place to linger.

EVERY ENTRY MUST HAVE AN APPROACH—a series of elements that create a smooth transition to your front door. Landings (or stoops) and porches fall into this category because they provide a resting place to gather the mail or get out the front door key.

The most simple landing can be a single stone step or fan of concrete before the front door. More elaborate examples include flights of steps leading to a landing, small decks, porches just large enough to protect the entry from inclement weather, and large porches that span the entire front of a house.

The more room for a landing, the more fun you can have with it. Some landings are big enough to furnish like an outdoor room, while others are tiny, with just enough space for a small accent, like an antique boot scraper.

▶ A REAL VICTORIAN PORCH makes an ideal outdoor living room. This gingerbread-trimmed example is painted in festive colors and furnished with rocking chairs and a wicker planter. Pots of hanging impatiens pick up colors in the trim.

▲ THIS LANDING in the corner of a broad porch is essentially transformed into an outdoor room, providing a comfortable resting spot for guests and visitors as well as an inviting space for homeowners to enjoy the outdoors. Cozy details include a rustic settee and chair, a side table, and shade-loving plants.

STEPS AND STOOPS

▲ SURROUNDED BY LOW FLOWERING shrubs and grasses, a few steps lead to a landing on an old stone house. The open landing, made of material the same color as the house, helps draw attention to the beautiful old façade.

▲ THIS ENTRY IS ENHANCED by a landing with interesting patterns. The outer bricks are turned on their sides, facing outward from the front door, while a diamond pattern is displayed on the inner part of the tread. Additional patterns are found in the railing, the door, and even the lantern.

▲ SOME FLORAL ACCENTS can be spontaneous, like this burst of bright purple ground cover growing right through the treads of a series of wide wood steps. Steps made of durable woods like cedar and mahogany make sense in temperate climates where freezing and thawing aren't much of an issue.

◄ THIS LANDING can be approached from two sides—an advantage given that the steps are open and unprotected, and that there is no handrail. The design is simple yet elegant—the steps seem to float as they rise up to the door.

◄ STEPS SHOULD BE CUT to a comfortable height for ease of use. Hard stones like granite make excellent choices in harsh, wintry climates because they don't crack or erode easily. Runs should be kept short; long flights of stone steps can be hazardous in wet or icy weather.

Stair Railings

STAIR RAILINGS ARE ESSENTIAL FOR **entry staircases with three or more steps. While you can make do with a sturdy metal handrail or a stock railing** from a builder's-supply or home store, the entry will look better if the railing is tailored to the rest of the trim on your house. There are companies that specialize in custom metal and wood railings, and you might be able to find a local artisan in your own community who can make your design.

A simple railing consists of a diagonal run of straight spindles held in place by top and bottom rails, affixed to posts at the top and the bottom of the stair. You can elaborate on the basic form by adding extra shaping or decorative millwork to any of the components.

If the railing will be made of wood, choose a durable, long-lived species like mahogany, and keep the wood sealed or painted to protect it from rot.

▲ AN ENTRY AT THE TOP of a long flight of stairs is an opportunity to add a decorative porch railing. In this case where the entry landing is raised over the garage, the railing is made up of narrowly spaced boards enhanced with cutwork diamonds.

► STAIR RAILINGS should reflect the style of the house. These massive posts and stout porch railings complement other architectural millwork on a high-style Victorian home. The steps, of poured concrete, are almost incidental to the design.

▶ WHENEVER THERE ARE TWO or more steps, it's a good idea to add at least one hand rail—preferably two—for safety. This Folk Victorian home has a rail on either side of the steps, making it easy for two people to reach the landing at a time.

◀ STEPS FACED WITH STONES suggest a rocky coastal environment. While stone is a traditional material for steps and stoops in New England and the mid-Atlantic, the use here is more decorative, with the stones embedded in concrete or cement.

COVERED ENTRIES

▶ A COVERED ENTRY can make a real statement on a house. This one gets its sense of presence from grouped pillars supporting a massive porch roof with a temple-like gable. Integral benches with stylish cutouts add a welcoming air.

▼ LOCATING A PERGOLA near an entry porch is a good option in a dry, sunny climate, where frequent downpours are not a problem. Plant climbing vines near the wood posts, and ultimately you will have a shade-covered sitting area.

► THERE IS NO better argument for a covered entry than snowy weather. If you live in a climate where the snow level can easily reach the porch landing, some kind of protection is a must.

▼ THIS COLUMNED PORCH projects well out from the front of the house, covering not only the entry but also the windows on either side. The style is a favorite in the South, where abundant light makes shade something to be desired.

▲ A COVERED ENTRY that is integrated into the roof-line can be an elegant piece of architecture. This one, supported by a simple tapered column, is covered by a shallow, undulating roof form known as an "eyebrow" curve.

Covering an Entry

Nothing creates curb appeal as quickly as a well-designed entry porch. Surprisingly, entry porches are far down the wish list of most-desired remodeling projects. Yet a welcoming entry porch almost automatically makes a house more appealing to guests or would-be buyers.

The simplest covered entry is one that protects only the front stoop. The roof can be a peaked gable (a and d) or a pitched shed style (b). (A gable roof has the extra advantage of diverting rain down the sides rather than the front like a shed roof.)

Even more desirable is a full front porch, extending across the full width of the house (c). A full porch creates extra usable space and makes the house appear much larger than it actually is.

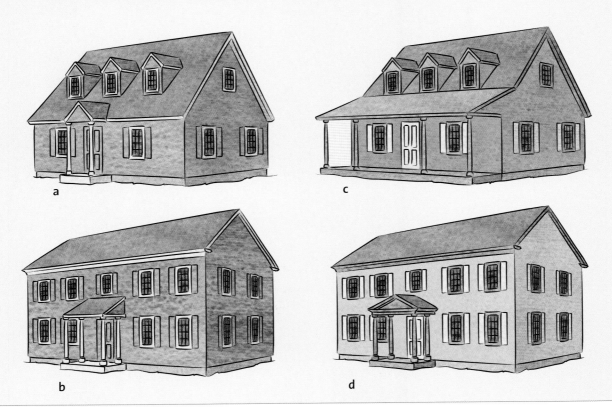

a

c

b

d

► LOW LANDINGS often lack architectural presence. This one gets added punch from a projecting, arched canopy and dramatically splayed pillars. The dark tropical wood on the landing and stair steps is not only durable, but it contrasts well with the white trim.

◄ WHEN A FRONT YARD is private, the approach to the entry can be almost as relaxed as a backyard patio. Here, low stone walls enclose a small courtyard, where there is enough space for a dining area and a bench under the porch.

▼ THE BIGGER THE PORCH, the more it becomes an extension of the house, literally adding square footage to the overall space of your home. This long, wide veranda is furnished with two sitting areas, including one with a table for dining or playing cards or board games.

◄ THE COVERED ENTRY on this recently remodeled Cape-style home plays off other architectural shapes on the house, notably the end gable and the dormer gables on the second story. The bumped-out rooflines give the house architectural relief, but the overall effect is harmonious.

PORCHES

▼ A COTTAGE-STYLE ENTRY set back on a deep porch is open and welcoming. To bring extra light into the house, the owner opted to install glass panes in and around the door, including the narrow side windows called sidelights.

▲ ▼ CHANGING THE ROOFLINE of the porch from a low flat extension to a wide, dramatic gable transformed the look of this home. Although the house is technically no bigger, it appears much more substantial thanks to the new peaked roof.

▲ THE ENTRY PORCH on this single-story Cape-style home extends across most of the front of the house, but the flat roof makes it look cramped and unappealing. The owners decided to rethink its shape as part of a cosmetic makeover.

▲ A COVERED PORCH can be useful on the side of the house, especially if there are entrances to guest quarters along the passage. Lighting should be spaced every few feet to ensure the entire length of the structure is well-lit.

▼ A PORCH THAT GETS several hours of sunlight daily is an ideal place to grow flowers. For best effect, place plants at different heights—low to the ground, at the windowsill, and hanging just beneath the porch roof—to create a cascade of foliage and blossoms.

▲ A PAIR OF CANE-BACK ROCKING CHAIRS adds instant appeal to any porch. Porches are also good places to display large pieces of pottery, often called jardinières. They can hold plants or simply be decorative, like this oversized example.

▲ WITH A BANK OF WINDOWS with paneled shutters as a backdrop, the owner of this attractive space has created a relaxing outdoor living room on the porch. Various pieces of wicker form a casual seating area around an indoor–outdoor rug.

▲ FULL-WIDTH PORCHES are a charming throwback to the past, and make a house seem more expansive. Think of the posts that support the porch roof as a decorating opportunity: Use columns or shaped posts, like the ones on this Neo-Victorian house.

◄ YOU CAN ADD CHARM to a porch with surprisingly few details. The accents here include a screen door painted red, a single painted rocker, and a fringe of gingerbread along the edge of the porch ceiling.

3

The Approach

The path to your front door should be a journey of small pleasures that appeals to the senses. Just think of neatly cropped grass bordering a meandering stone walkway, the scent of blooming roses in well-tended planting beds, or the rustle of leaves from a nearby stand of trees. Such sights, smells, and sounds will leave a good and lasting impression to visitors and passersby.

Even if your yard is the standard-issue rectangle of grass with shrubbery hugging the foundation of the house, try to envision it as a landscape that you can shape. Begin by assessing your site and looking for ways to enhance it. Is the grass healthy and green? Are the plants in the yard about the right size and scale or are they overgrown or nonexistent? Is there an attractive path that leads guests to the front door?

Consider both the limitations and possibilities of your front yard, and select materials and plants that best suit the climate and your degree of interest in gardening and lawn maintenance. The key elements to consider for maximum impact are landscaping plants (including grass, flowers, ground covers, shrubbery, and trees), paths and walkways, and one aspect you might have overlooked—outdoor lighting.

◄ THIS HOUSE ALREADY HAS STORYBOOK APPEAL, but the landscape sets the stage for it. A brick path winds its way to the front door through a well-kept lawn and lush beds of flowering plants and ornamental trees.

Shaping the Landscape

THERE ARE AN INFINITE NUMBER OF WAYS to shape and define your home landscape. While an expanse of healthy grass can make a front yard appealing, so can a terraced hill landscaped with stones, retaining walls, and shrubbery, or a "dry" front yard with drought-resistant plants and beds of stone or rock.

Begin by evaluating your site. Is the grass in good shape? Are the foundation plants ragged? Next, think about what you'd like your front yard to become. Should you add shade trees, beds of flowers, or a new pathway? Some approaches require a lot of maintenance, but that's not a problem if you can afford regular landscape care or if you're ready to do the work yourself.

▲ GRASS CAN MAKE A LOVELY front landscape, particularly if your house is painted white. Keep the lawn mowed regularly, and remove the clippings when you cut so that thatch doesn't build up and smother new growth.

◄ A CURVING BRICK PATH trimmed with stone not only creates a clear passage to the front of this house but also gives shape and definition to planting beds on either side of the passage. A bonus: There's little grass to cut.

▲ THIS FRONT YARD is particularly welcoming due to the charming flower garden enclosed by a white picket fence. Visitors enter the garden by stepping in between peaked-roof posts that double as tiny birdhouses.

Assessing Your Site

BEFORE YOU BEGIN re-creating your front yard, get out some graph paper and a 25-ft. measuring tape and create a site plan. Draw a sketch of the property boundaries and the placement of the house roughly to scale (measure widths and distances between the house and other features like the driveway and large trees). Then locate the key landscaping elements in your yard on the sketch.

Stand at the edge of the yard with the sketch in hand. What's missing? What needs to be replaced? Should you add an ornamental tree surrounded by flower beds on one side of the yard, or replace a concrete path with a brick one?

Consider the results from a three-dimensional perspective; the most pleasant yards include landscaping elements that vary in height and texture.

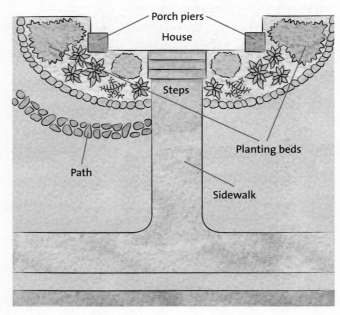

▲ A BUNGALOW PORCH IS TRIMMED with neat circular planting beds that seem to flow around the massive stone pillars supporting the roof. The vegetation not only softens the line between the house and the yard but also extends the welcome out into the yard.

◄ ONE OF THE MOST EFFECTIVE WAYS to use foundation shrubs is to plant them in successive tiers, with shorter shrubs in front of taller ones. This technique creates visual interest, allowing you to see a variety of foliage at different levels. Here, evergreens make a pleasing backdrop for banks of flowering hydrangeas.

▲ PORCHES ARE transitional spaces that should be welcoming and restful—characteristics that should be apparent whether you're coming from inside the house or from the front yard. Here, a pair of comfortable and colorful Adirondack chairs invites visitors to linger.

◄ ANOTHER ATTRACTIVE WAY to incorporate a covered entry is to recess it underneath second-story living space. This one on the corner of a house with a steeply pitched roof is easily accessible to the driveway, front yard, and side patio, thanks to broad steps that wrap around the landing.

▲ IF YOUR YARD is especially spacious, edge a walk with a deep bed of plants that vary in height, color, size, and texture. Position low ground covers nearest the path, with plants that will create the most spectacular show in the middle or rear of the bed.

▶ POTTED BOXWOOD TOPIARIES and a leafy climbing clematis soften a small brick courtyard leading to a formal front door. Without the plantings to break up the many hard surfaces, the approach would seem cold and stark.

Using Plants Effectively

FOLLOW THESE GUIDELINES to create a front yard with appealing landscaping.

- Choose plants that are easy to grow and maintain.

- Make sure your plants suit both the soil and the amount of light the yard receives. In many states, you can have the soil tested by a local agricultural agent for factors like alkalinity and nitrogen content. If the yard is sunny, you'll be able to choose from a wide variety of plants and flowers; if it's shady, you'll need to look for shade-loving varieties.

- Create visual interest and vary textures by "layering" plants. Put the tallest specimens at the back and the lowest in the front.

- Choose plants that offer a lot of variation in foliage and range of color (light and variegated greens to deep glossy greens).

- Look for species that offer changes from season to season. Boston ivy, for example, offers green foliage in spring, berries in summer, red foliage in fall, and interesting vine patterns in winter.

▲ THE PATH TO THE FRONT DOOR can be attractive without being a blank slate of newly mown grass. Low, brushy ground cover, flowering shrubs, and a climbing vine with dark, glossy leaves make a soft, inviting frame for this doorway.

◄ THIS HOME USES the hillside landscape to create a welcoming trip to the front door. A walkway of mixed materials creates visual interest and the landings between the steps allow guests to enjoy the native plantings.

FLOWERS AND FOLIAGE

▲ WINDOW BOXES ARE A GREAT WAY to soften the line between your house and the front landscape. Window-box plantings, which can be changed seasonally, provide a bright burst of accent color to the front of your house.

▲ FLOWERS AREN'T THE ONLY WAY to add color to your landscape. Mixing plants with leaves of different colors and textures is one of the best ways to keep your landscape interesting all year, especially if the plants are massed for a graduated effect.

▶ EVEN IF THE "LAWN" IS COVERED with a visually appealing pattern of brick, you can still create a diverse landscape with potted plants that vary in terms of leaf shapes, sizes, flowers, and colors. Be sure to add some seating, too, so visitors can pause to enjoy the display.

▲ INCORPORATE WALLS and other hardscape features as part of a plan to edge or layer plants for dramatic effect. A bed of flowering purple flowers explodes with color against a low stone wall of flat, beige boulders.

◄ TWO DIFFERENT VARIETIES of hydrangea—one purplish blue, the other white—are massed against each other to create a stunning summer display. To maintain visual interest at other times of the year, mix in ornamental shrubs that shine in other seasons, such as pyracantha or holly.

► A LOW ADOBE-RED WALL and brilliant desert flowers and cactus highlight the approach to a Spanish Colonial style house in Arizona. Incorporating plant species that are native to your area will usually reward you with ease of care and bursts of color in spring and summer.

IN THE DETAILS

Adding a Fountain

WATER FEATURES tend to have a soothing effect—a good reason to add one if your intention is to make your yard a relaxing retreat.

Small fountains are often sold with all the parts you need to set them up. A fountain kit consists of a basin to hold the water and a decorative spout or vessel that conceals the tube that funnels water into the basin. A small internal pump shoots the water through the fountain; in most cases, the water recirculates. You only need to refill the basin as water evaporates. Most fountains run on electricity, so you'll either need to have a power outlet close at hand or be prepared to dig a trench for a grounded line.

Fountains can be made of almost any material, including stone, concrete, and metals like copper and steel. They also can be highly decorative—almost like a sculpture.

► THE SOFT, GURGLING SOUNDS of moving water has a soothing effect. That explains why fountains appeal to the senses. Here, water streams from an old tin watering can-turned-fountain into a waiting basin. Even a small fountain helps circulate air and adds moisture to a garden.

▲ A SMALL FRONT YARD is a great place to experiment with flowering plants and grasses. Allow ample room for a pathway like this jagged flagstone walk, and choose flowering species, grasses, and ground covers geared toward the amount of light the area receives, whether sunny or shady.

◄ COTTAGE-STYLE GARDENS are often a riot of overgrown plants and flowers with no grass in sight. This one maintains a bit of order, however, thanks to a wood fence and a wide gate topped with a pergola.

Color Combinations

CREATING GREAT-LOOKING PLANT combinations is easier said than done. While it might seem logical to use two flowers of the same color together, for instance, they might not actually complement each other if one is a hot version of that color and one is cool. Have fun planting flowers together but realize that it might take some trial and error to get just the right combination. Here are some ideas to get you started.

▲ New Guinea impatiens, caladium, and green dragon aroid.

▲ Globe amaranth, tropical smoke bush, and flowering tobacco.

▲ Mealycup sage, zinnia, and coneflower.

▲ Purple shamrock, ornamental pepper, impatiens, and heliotrope.

▲ Pacific hybrid delphiniums, Asiatic lily, and ligularia.

▲ CREATE A SHOW OF COLOR with blooming plants that come in an array of pastels, like impatiens, petunias, or azaleas. Group them in single-color beds, or mix and match colors to create beds with high contrast (i.e., red and white) or graduated colors (white, pink, and fuchsia, for example).

◄ EVEN WHEN YOUR HOME is a row house right on the street and sidewalk, there is always room for flowers. A long built-in planter under a bank of windows on the third floor provides a show of color all summer long.

Walks and Paths

THE PATH TO YOUR FRONT DOOR may cover a small amount of ground, but it has a big impact on the overall appeal of your yard. Like the entry, a front walk should be a focal point—functional, easy to see, and a pleasure to use. While there's nothing wrong with a path that marches straight through the yard to the entry, front walks can also bend or zigzag with the terrain or gently curve through or around other features in the yard, such as flower beds or stands of trees.

Almost any material that drains well and stands up to the weather can make a good front walkway, including gravel, concrete, brick, and stone. Although the surface should provide good footing in all kinds of weather (especially when it's icy or wet), it should have visual interest, too.

▲ TO CREATE A WALK that's visually interesting, use more than one paving material. The concrete sections in this path stand out like a dashed line in a bed of earth-colored brick, making the path easier to read; it's also easier to see at dusk.

◄ STONE LAID IN A formal pattern makes a beeline to a guest house across this patch of smooth lawn. The side path is far less formal: The two irregularly shaped stones suggest stepping stones in a "pond" of grass.

◄ A BRICK PATH adds a sense of order to a riot of roses, flowering shrubs, and ground cover in this cottage-style garden. Brick lasts a long time, has an interesting texture, and its variable coloring makes a pleasing contrast for growing plants.

▼ THIS STONE PATH makes its way through a hillside garden. To create a walkway on a slope requires minor excavation: You'll need to level the soil for the steps as the hill gradually rises. Plant a year-round ground cover such as pachysandra or creeping myrtle on either side of the steps to minimize erosion.

◄ IF YOUR YARD has a sharp drop or a creek running through it, a raised walkway is one method of keeping the path to the front door relatively flat and dry. This one, made of weather-resistant decking material, includes lighting along the railing for a safe approach at night.

▲ FORMAL ENTRIES are often symmetrical. This house with its central entry and windows balanced on either side calls out for a front path that's centered on the front door. Even the bricks themselves emphasize the formal design: They are laid so that they line up with the entry.

► CONCRETE WALKS can be dressed up or disguised in any number of ways. This walk features a pattern of cracks that makes it look like flagstone. Although today's concrete can be tinted or made to look like stone, it's easier to create a new look when the material is freshly mixed and laid.

◄ NATURAL STONE PAVERS in a repeating pattern follow a curving path from a trellised arbor to the front porch. The surface of the pavers has a lot of texture, which makes them easier to walk on when the ground is wet or icy.

▼ THIS TINY BEACH COTTAGE in town uses the sidewalk to welcome guests to the front door. Colorful, spreading plants break through the hard lines of the fence.

BRICK

◄ COMBINING DIFFERENT PATTERNS and colors of brick can add a lot of interest to a path. This walk, which creates a cul de sac with a tree as its focal point, incorporates several shades of brick and two kinds of edging.

▼ ALLOW A GENEROUS AMOUNT of room for planting beds or grass between your home and any path that parallels it. Here, dense foliage softens the transition between the brick walk, laid in a herringbone pattern, and the house.

▲ BRICK WALKS ALMOST ALWAYS have borders to give them a crisp edge. This series of intersecting walks in a running bond pattern is trimmed with the most common edging pattern—a straight line of bricks laid perpendicular to the main run of the walk.

Brick Walks

THERE ARE HUNDREDS OF VARIATIONS of brick patterns for walks. Some of the most common are running bond, basket weave, herringbone, and diagonal. Any of these patterns, properly laid, will reward you with an attractive, durable path for years to come.

Laying a brick walk can be hard work, but it isn't hard to do. Begin by excavating a bed at least 4 in. deeper than the depth of the pavers you intend to use. Fill the bed with a 4-in. layer of stone dust. Tamp the dust down and mist it with water. Then begin laying your pavers, beginning with the border. (Use hard-fired paving brick—not old bricks left over from a construction site—or parts of your walk may begin to crack or crumble after a few seasons.) Pack the bricks in tightly, and tamp down with a mallet.

To trim a brick to fit, use a brick set, a broad-bladed masonry chisel, and the mallet. When you need to make a cut, draw a line across the edge of the brick where you want to remove excess material. Hold the edge of the brick set firmly on the line with the beveled side away from the part of the brick you intend to use. Strike the tool firmly with the mallet, and it should break cleanly.

Once the pattern is laid, fill in the cracks with more stone dust to prevent grass from gaining a foothold, then mist with a hose to set it. (You may want to repeat this process once the dust has had time to settle.)

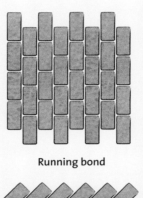
Running bond

Herringbone

Diagonal

Basket weave

▲ AN ATTRACTIVE PAVED AREA like this driveway set with brick pavers can lead naturally into a front walkway. Creating one continuous surface also helps establish and define planting areas for a show of seasonal color.

▲ THIS PATH IS ACTUALLY A SERIES of stepping stones with a novel twist. These footsteps are composed of multiple bricks in a herringbone pattern. Although the effect is traditional, the path is anything but ordinary.

STONE

▶ A COVERED WALK THAT SETS OFF a raked Japanese garden is paved with cut pieces of thin, evenly layered stone called flagstone. Although flagstone makes an elegant and durable walk, the material tends to be expensive. A more affordable alternative is concrete that's made to look like stone.

▲ THIS RAMBLING PATH makes use of locally available stones such as granite and irregularly shaped flagstone. To keep grass from creeping in, fill in cracks and crevices between larger stones with crushed rock or chipped gravel, or plant a fragrant, low-growing ground cover such as creeping thyme.

▶ BRICK, STONE, AND GRAVEL aren't the only materials for paths and walkways. If your budget allows, add drama with unusual materials and textures. Here, a side path of rubbed stones leads to a formal walk of tile in a checkerboard pattern.

▲ HARD, ALMOST IMPENETRABLE stones like granite will serve long and well as steps cut into the side of a hill, even in a harsh climate. This retaining wall is dry-stacked, meaning each stone is laid in place by hand without mortar, creating a more natural look for the wall.

► SQUARE, BLOCKY PAVERS set in mortar are laid with free-form edges in this garden path. The unusual edge treatment and the irregular path of the walk suggest a rocky river overflowing its banks, a nice touch in a garden without grass or lush plantings.

► STONE PAVERS work well with other materials: In this Asian-inspired courtyard, the pavers combine with a wide boardwalk to create a serene mood. Laying the boards perpendicular to the pavers allows the texture of both materials to stand out.

▼ BECAUSE CUT FLAGSTONE is available in squares and rectangles of different sizes, it lends itself to interesting patterns for walks and paths. This composition gets an extra jolt of color from the use of brick squares as accents.

► A PATH OF LIGHT-COLORED flagstone meanders through this colorful summer flower garden. The gaps between the stones have been allowed to fill in with a low, creeping ground cover, which adds extra texture and contrast to the path.

▼ A SHORT FLIGHT OF STONE STEPS centered on the front door of a Colonial-era house abruptly ends when it reaches the lawn, suggesting that its original purpose—as a stop for carriages—is long gone. Now it's just an intriguing feature that draws the eye to the front door.

▲ LARGE PIECES OF FLAGSTONE make a wide, enduring divider between stands of grasses and flowers, both of which help to soften the sharp edges of the stone. Cut stone is one of the most expensive materials for walkways, but it lasts far longer and needs less care than gravel or mulch.

Lighting the Landscape

While it's important to light paths, steps, doorways, and driveways for visibility and safety reasons, lighting can also enhance your home's curb appeal by adding a sense of drama, especially at night.

Choose outdoor fixtures that direct light either up, down, or to one side. Uplights in or near the ground make sense when you want to accent a tree or cast light on the front of the house. Downlights are an alternative if you want to illuminate a path from above or spotlight a side yard with lighting recessed into an eave.

Unless the light fixture is especially attractive, try to conceal or minimize it. You want to emphasize the stone path or that lovely specimen tree, not the high-tech-looking fixture mounted on a post or staked in the ground. Used skillfully, outdoor lighting can make your home safe and beautiful.

▲ FOOTLIGHTS RECESSED into low stone walls that flank nearby steps are a great safety feature in snowy climates. These fixtures cast light directly on the steps, while a pair of hanging downlights illuminates the landing.

◀ LARGE LANTERNS on either side of this doorway cast warm ambient light, but they don't do much to illuminate the large covered entryway. They get some help, however, from a concealed light mounted on one of the beams that span the entry roof.

▲ CONCEALED DOWNLIGHTS give a big boost to a pendant light in the entry of this rustic fishing lodge. While the entry light is large and attractive, most of the illumination actually comes from lights recessed in the eaves and porch ceiling.

▲ LIGHTED POSTS, which cast illumination sideways and downward, are an effective way to light the passage into a driveway or parking area. These attractive lanterns are mounted on low tapered piers finished with shingles that complement the shingle siding on the garage and the main house.

LIGHTING PATHS AND WALKWAYS

◄ A COLONIAL-STYLE post lantern is well suited to this mid-20th-century house in the same style. While the single post light casts enough illumination for a relatively short path, a longer walkway would require a series of fixtures so that the pools of light overlap and illuminate the entire length of the walk.

► UNLESS THEY'RE especially handsome, exterior light fixtures should not be visible in the daytime. This lamp on the entry wall is the only fixture with a lot of visibility in a yard filled with small, discreet lights. At night, the lantern "calls out" the stone wall and illuminates its interesting texture.

▲ A LIGHT CAN SERVE more than one purpose, particularly if it's attractive. This Japanese-inspired wood-and-copper lantern not only highlights the turn-in for a driveway, but also it makes a nice focal point for a low stone wall.

▲ A RAISED WALKWAY gets plenty of illumination from small sconces mounted at foot level. The tiny footlights, which are fairly easy to install, make an evening passage along the walk a safe and pleasant experience.

Low-Voltage Lighting Systems

LOW-VOLTAGE LIGHTS are a great way to put light right where you want it in your yard. Use them to illuminate paths, steps, and walkways as accent lighting or for low-level general illumination. The fixtures run off a transformer that plugs into a standard wall outlet, ramping down the standard 120-volt energy flow to a mere 12 volts.

The small, compact lights are linked together by 12-gauge wire cable, which runs along the ground. It's a good idea to make sure the cable is placed in areas where it isn't likely to be disturbed, such as under shrubs or along fences. The lights can be mounted on posts, staked in the ground, or concealed in shrubbery or planting beds.

Like other forms of exterior lighting, low-voltage lights can point up or down to draw attention to a specimen tree or a special feature of your home, like a fountain. You can also use them as backlights to create a silhouette effect. Despite their low voltage, these lights are exceptionally bright, so make sure you use them sparingly to target specific features.

The lights can be activated by a number of means, including timers and photoelectric cells that generate light after dark. While the components for a low-voltage system are relatively inexpensive (a small kit costs only a few hundred dollars), it's best to have your outdoor lighting installed by a landscaping professional experienced with these kinds of systems.

▲ LOW-VOLTAGE LIGHTING installed along the path to a front door provides illumination for nighttime visitors. The up-facing lights also cast dramatic accent lighting on both the entry and the crape myrtle trees that line the walk.

▲ HARDWIRED EXTERIOR LIGHTING must be installed by an electrician and meet local electrical codes, usually making it a more expensive choice than low-voltage lighting. But hardwiring is a must for lights at the end of a long run from the power source, such as this driveway fixture.

▲ THE LONG ENTRY CORRIDOR for this factory-built house is illuminated with sconces mounted high on the wall, just under the porch roof. Although wall-mounted fixtures work just as well as lights mounted in the eaves, they should be attractive, since they'll be visible day and night.

◄ WHENEVER A WALKWAY intersects with an element like a stone wall, it's a good idea to add lighting for safety reasons. The light not only keeps visitors from bumping into the wall, but it also helps define the transition from a more public space into a more private one.

4

Decks

Decks are relatively new arrivals to residential architecture; prior to the 1930s houses had either porches or patios for the purpose of outdoor relaxation and entertainment. Simply defined, decks are room-shaped floors without walls or ceilings—a man-made landscape, generally located on the back or most private side of a house, which extends its footprint.

Decks can hug the ground or float like treehouses, and range from simple rectangular platforms to multilevel structures with complex architectural details. When planning a deck, it's important to integrate it into the landscape while complementing the house, so shape, materials, and plantings should be considered carefully.

And a deck should receive the same thoughtful outfitting as an indoor room; depending on the atmosphere you wish to achieve, it can simply house a couple of deck chairs (what else!), or it can be a full-blown room with all the amenities.

◄ WHEN THE OWNERS OF THIS LARGE HOME did a major renovation in the Craftsman style, decks and stonework were added, creating both visual interest and useful outdoor space. By making the lower corner posts larger than those in the balustrade, a visual hierarchy and pleasing sense of rhythm are established, which also break up the mass of the house behind.

Deck Types

WHETHER YOU DESIRE A PRIVATE DECK off an upper-level bedroom, a wraparound party deck with a view of the ocean, or a children's play deck off the family room, certain considerations must inform your planning. The shape and style of your home and the size and orientation of your property will be the primary determinants when deciding on the type of deck you build, and a well-designed deck takes advantage of what a home already has to offer.

Although decks come in all shapes, sizes, and levels, there are five basic categories: platform decks, raised decks, second-story decks, multi-level decks, and freestanding decks (see the illustration on p. 102). Angular, geometric shapes are easiest to build, but curved decks are possible, though they must be planned carefully and are more costly.

▼BUILDING CURVES INTO A DECK takes more time and labor, and thus costs more, but the results can be spectacular, as witnessed by this multi-level redwood deck. The decking is 2x6 redwood boards, and the serpentine railing is made up of thin strips that can be bent easily.

▲THIS RAISED DECK CAPITALIZES on a stunning panoramic view, and the horizontal cables in the railing cleverly echo the horizon line without blocking it. Sturdy deck materials and furnishings were selected for this seaside meadow site to withstand the winter squalls.

◀AMBIENT LIGHT from the house's large windows spills out onto this simple platform deck with chairs perfectly positioned to watch the sun set over the water. That might be all you want for exterior lights, especially in a natural setting like this one where a lack of pollution allows the stars to be a twinkling centerpiece at night.

DECK SHAPES

▲DESIGNED FOR ENTERTAINING, this angular free-standing deck has a multitude of components: a sunken spa, outdoor kitchen, lattice fence, and built-in benches and planters. Redwood is a good choice for a large deck that is a whole play area because of its natural durability.

▶THE ROUNDED EDGE OF THIS ALLURING DECK is repeated in the cascading steps that lead down to the lawn, lending it an unusual shape reminiscent of a small man-made hillock tucked up against the house. Ringing a deck with steps lets you forgo the use of a continuous guardrail around it, allowing an uninterrupted view.

▲▼ THIS COMMODIOUS AND CURVY DECK made of ipe seems to set sail into the landscape, offering a much more interesting silhouette than a straight deck would. The underside of the deck is hidden from view by a continuous wooden skirt that conceals the deck's structure, hiding the posts and joists within the graceful curve. The sinuous railing—with a balustrade of wrought-iron panels between rhythmic posts—accentuates the shape of the deck.

DECK TYPES

Any deck is a unique construction, custom designed and built for a particular house and to meet particular needs of the homeowners. The basic types of decks shown here are general categories to help in planning the type of deck that suits location and usage.

PLATFORM DECKS
Low to the ground; no need for railings or steps; can take any shape.

RAISED DECKS
Raised a few steps above the ground; require protective railings and steps to grade.

ROOFTOP DECKS
Set on top of a flat-roofed portion of the house; require careful installation to maintain waterproof roofing.

SECOND-STORY DECKS
A deck that's a full story above the ground; may or may not have stairs to the yard.

POOLSIDE DECKS
Extend around inground or above-ground pools; may incorporate a building code-required fence.

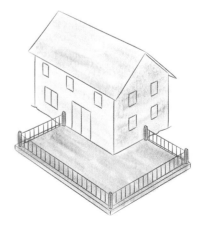

WRAPAROUND DECKS
Any deck that takes a turn around a corner of the house.

CREATING A COUNTERPOINT to the rounded wall of the house, this platform deck takes the straight tack, with a bump-out at the apex of the curve for visual drama and a seating area. The narrow section of the deck outside the curved windows is left free from embellishments that would block the view from inside.

▲ THIS EMBRACING, WRAPAROUND DECK blurs the distinctions between front, side, and back, creating for the house a sense of fluid location in the landscape while taking advantage of the multiple views. Making the deck entrance a natural continuation of the grassy path leading to it further enhances the deck's organic feel.

▲ FANCIFUL FAT COLUMNS stand sentry at this deck that's built low to the ground in the crook of a house with many nautical references (the owner wanted to mimic a tugboat). The belly of the column is repeated in the shapes of the house and the outward-swelling balusters on the second-floor deck.

▶ DESIGNED IN CONCERT with the house, rather than tacked on as an afterthought, this unusually shaped deck is the result of a limited site and the desire to capture as much daylight and passive solar radiation as possible. The curve of the south-facing deck hugs the house, making it an extension of the living space inside.

◄THIS HOUSE BOASTS TWO UPPER-STORY triangular decks that jut out into the air like arrowheads, embracing the landscape and view. To maintain unobstructed views from the lower-level family rooms, each deck is designed to be supported by one main post.

◄AROUND THE CORNER from the triangular decks, the sawtooth edge of the house is juxtaposed to this straight shot of deck. The planking is laid on the long direction, accentuating the length of the deck and forming mini-rooms within the crooks of the building.

►LAYING DECK PLANKING on the diagonal is a dynamic alternative to orienting the planking parallel or perpendicular to the house. Here, the resulting sawtooth edge of this raised deck creates interesting nooks to house seats or plantings.

DECKING PATTERNS

The direction and pattern that the decking takes starts with the layout of the supporting framing. The simplest pattern is to lay decking at 90 degrees to the framing, making sure that seams between the ends of the planks fall over framing below. Diagonal decking patterns, curved edges, and basketweave patterns require more framing beneath.

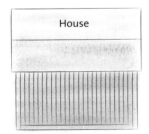

Perpendicular to the house

Parallel to the house

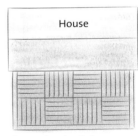

Diagonal

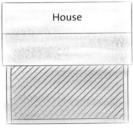

Parquet or basketweave

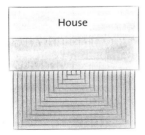

Herringbone

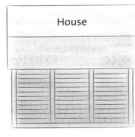

Sectional

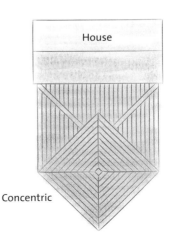

Concentric

◀▲THIS SPACIOUS, RAISED DECK is perfect for entertaining, with its multiple lengths converging in the circular seating and eating area, which is further distinguished from the rest of the deck with an eye-catching, concentric decking pattern. The vertical skirting mimics the siding on the house, creating natural flow between the structures.

▲SHORT PLANKS CAN BE REPLACED easily if they show signs of rot, especially in a pool/hot tub area like this where there will be lots of water splashed on the deck.

▲REDWOOD MAKES A BEAUTIFUL, durable, and stable material for this contemporary multilevel deck with brushed stainless steel rails. To preserve redwood decking, a protective finish that contains mildewcides, water repellents, and ultraviolet protection should be applied every few years.

►THIS MAHOGANY DECK is built within a concrete wall that forms a substantial edge under the deck. The vibrant painted coping (covering) at the deck's edge acts as a visual transition between the natural wood and boisterous metal railing, which lends a casual playfulness to the structure. Narrow spaces between the decking planks accommodate wood's tendency to expand in warm weather and obscure uneven shrinking as the deck ages.

Choosing Deck Materials

A VARIETY OF DECKING MATERIALS are available, from domestic wood species to tropical hardwoods to synthetics and vinyl products. Price, availability, quality, and environmental concerns will affect your selection. Getting samples of the ones you're considering will help make your choice easier.

- PRESSURE-TREATED WOOD is the least expensive, and one of the most popular, options. It's usually made of fir, southern pine, or hemlock (or some combination of hemlock and fir). Pressure-treated woods have a greenish-brown hue but can be stained if you find that unappealing. Be aware that the chemicals that make it rot-resistant include a type of arsenic. (This type of treatment is being phased out of use.) Although pressure-treated wood is safe to touch and doesn't leach into the ground, wear safety goggles and gloves if you are working with it, and never burn it.

- SOFTWOODS like cedar and redwood are beautiful and naturally rot- and decay-resistant, but they're more expensive than treated wood. Cedar is available in two species—western red cedar and Alaska cedar. Western red is reddish-brown and lighter and softer than Alaska yellow cedar or redwood. Yellow cedar has a clear, pale yellowish color, which weathers to silver-gray. Redwood, renowned for its rich hue, is very easy to work with and holds finish well.

- TROPICAL HARDWOODS, such as mahogany, ipe, and meranti, are a luxurious option and extremely durable and resistant to rot and insect damage. However, they're expensive and can be difficult to work with.

- SYNTHETIC WOOD PLANKING is an environmentally conscientious alternative to real wood and is splinter-free. However, synthetics are too weak to be used as structural framing and are used only for decking. Unlike wood, which requires a protective sealer every year, synthetics need virtually no maintenance but are more expensive. Synthetics come in several forms: Composite materials, such as Trex®, are made of recycled plastics and wood fibers, and vinyl decking is made from PVC.

▲ A SAMPLE OF DECKING MATERIALS (from left to right): treated southern pine, redwood, Brock Deck® vinyl decking, pressure-treated fir, Trex® plastic composite decking, Nexwood™ plastic composite, ipe, Dream Deck vinyl decking.

▲ TREX® IS A POPULAR SYNTHETIC COMPOSITE decking and railing material made of recycled plastic and wood fibers. Splinter-free and moisture-resistant, it comes in several colors, and because it curves more easily than wood, it can be a good material to use for building curved decks and railings such as this one.

▶ PREMIUM DECKING MATERIALS, such as the redwood shown here, can take on a furniture-like appearance when well cared for, and the decorative wood accents inserted into the decking pattern enhance that effect. A concealed fastening system was used, which keeps the decking unmarred by nail heads.

Deck Maintenance

PROPERLY FINISHING AND MAINTAINING a deck surface will prevent staining and rot and will keep it structurally sound and looking good for a long time.

Some wood species, like cedar and redwood, have natural water- and rot-resistant properties and can be left unfinished to turn a lovely silver over time. Most other woods must be finished with either a clear or semitransparent stain. These finishes will repel water, and some contain preservatives: fungicides, mildewcides, and insecticides. Pigmented stains and finishes also act as sunscreens and will help the wood retain its color.

Finishes must be reapplied every year or two to maintain the deck surface. Sweep, wash, and bleach if necessary between finish treatments, allowing the deck to dry thoroughly before applying the first coat of the finish.

Railings, Stairs, and Built-Ins

I N TERMS OF FUNCTIONALITY, safety, and aesthetics, railings and stairs are critical components of a deck and should be carefully designed. Both have detailed building code requirements, which vary by location and which will affect design, but with all the options now available, there's plenty of room for creativity. Railings can be made of a range of materials, from the traditional wood and metal to the more innovative glass and even mesh or netting. Stairs can take a variety of forms and be made from a number of materials as well to create interest while acting as a transitional element between deck and landscape. Built-in seating, planters, and storage are functional features that, when artfully constructed, can add some architectural spark to a deck. If substantial enough, they can also do double duty as railings.

▼LIKE A WHITE PICKET FENCE, this fresh white railing helps create the sense of a garden room. While railing components like these fancy finials add substantial style to a deck, they can be easily purchased at a lumberyard or home center and are relatively inexpensive.

▲ BUILT-IN PLANTERS AND BENCHES furnish this outdoor room under an open-air ceiling. As an extension
of the living room, this deck mimics the layout inside
with a planter serving as the outdoor alternative to a
corner table flanked by wooden "sofas."

◄ VARIOUS CONSIDERATIONS, from drainage concerns to
capitalizing on a good view, may mandate that a deck
be elevated, like this dramatic wraparound. While building codes govern all stairs and railings, they tend to be
more specific when applied to elevated structures; for
instance, codes restrict the amount of steps in a single
run, so rather than a continuous descent on this stair,
an intermediate landing has been incorporated.

RAILINGS

▲LYRICAL LIMBS FILL IN THE BALUSTRADE of this railing, and the shapes between the branches create unusually framed views of the trees and water. Peeled branches should be sanded to avoid splinters and sealed to maintain their original color.

▶WOOD RAILINGS HAVE A NUMBER of advantages: They are pleasant to grip even in very hot or cold weather, can take on a variety of profiles, are suitable for older homes, and can offer historic styling. Here the same rail is used in the second-floor pocket deck as on the long deck, bringing visual harmony to the two parts of the house.

Defining Railings

THE TERM "RAILING" is used interchangeably, but depending on where the railing falls, it is either a guardrail or a handrail. Building codes make this distinction clear in the regulations that apply to each. Check your local building code for specific requirements.

Guardrails surround a raised deck and are commonly 36 in. above the deck floor. Handrails follow alongside a stairway, with their height measured vertically from the nosing (the outer edge of the step's overhang) so that it falls within a range prescribed by building codes, generally about 32 in. to 36 in. Handrails must have a graspable profile to grip while climbing the stair, whereas guardrails need not be designed for gripping.

The area between the railings and deck or stairway is the balustrade and may be composed of closely spaced horizontal or vertical members, or it can be built as a low, solid wall, sometimes termed a knee wall. Knee walls must include scuppers—gaps for the water to drain out.

The spacing of the individual balusters must be close enough to prevent a 4-in.-diameter or larger ball from passing through. The gap between the balustrade and the steps cannot be larger than a 6-in.-diameter ball.

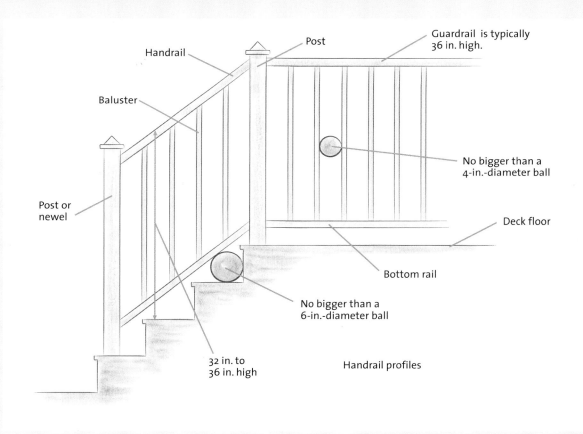

Handrail

Post

Baluster

Guardrail is typically 36 in. high.

Post or newel

No bigger than a 4-in.-diameter ball

Deck floor

Bottom rail

No bigger than a 6-in.-diameter ball

32 in. to 36 in. high

Handrail profiles

►SHAPED LIKE THE BATTLEMENTS of a castle, this deck features solidly shingled corners interspersed with a wood railing. The corners anchor the railing system visually as well as structurally, making it especially sturdy, which is critical for second-level decks.

►NATURAL WOOD RAILINGS would look too heavy and create too much contrast with this white-washed home, so they've been painted. Cedar or pressure-treated lumber is typically used for painted railings, and maintenance is key; you don't want water to stand on painted wood, so slant the top rail a little (as was done here) if it is made of a single plank, or shape the top of the rail to shed water.

Wood Balustrade Designs

THERE IS AN UNLIMITED VARIETY of designs for wood balustrades, which can add distinctive style to any deck. As long as the spacing between the balusters meets building code requirements, the pieces can be placed vertically, horizontally, or on the diagonal. Balustrades can be made of individual 1½-in. by 1½-in. balusters set in a row or be arranged with more ornate turned balusters or boards cut with a decorative profile. Balustrades are constructed in sections between upright posts that secure the balustrade to the deck framing. These look best and are sturdier when there is no more than 8 ft. of balustrade between posts.

◄ THE ALTERNATING RHYTHM to this railing must be planned in advance so that the design fits into the length of the railing; an abrupt ending in the middle of one of the H-shaped panels would look like a mistake. This holds true for any deck that has a row of individual panels.

►CURVED TOP AND BOTTOM RAILINGS formed of short sections of wood plank follow the gentle curve of this second-story deck that extends this home's footprint toward the water. Tying the ends in to the posts holding up the roof makes the railing more secure.

▼DESIGNED BY A CARPENTER for his own home, this railing frame is made of clear cedar and the spindles are ½-in. black pipe held in place with wooden dowels. With few exposed fasteners, there are fewer places for staining and rotting.

◄EQUALLY SPACED POSTS and balustrade panels with a medallion of sorts add a little spice to this railing pattern. The white rail contrasts with the vivid blues and greens of the natural surroundings and the pink and purple palette of the plants.

◄GOING BEYOND STRICT geometric shapes, this raised deck undulates above a supporting stone wall, forming pockets to stand within and view the terrain below. The sinuous railing echoes the deck's curve but is given further architectural interest through the profile of the balusters, which undulate vertically.

BALUSTERS

Taking a cue from more decorative porch railings, the individual balusters that make up a deck's balustrade need not be just simple 2x2s.

1½ in. x
1½ in. square

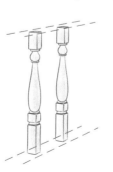

Turned

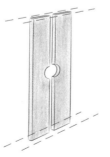

Set flat with decorative cutouts

Cut with a curvy profile from 2x6 boards

►USING A SOLID WALL AS RAILING makes a deck feel like part of the house—more like a porch without a roof. This railing is faced with the same clapboard and white trim as the house.

▼THIS HARMONIOUSLY DESIGNED deck features a solid railing made of the same shingled siding as that on the house, and the tapered columns are consistent with the prominent roof angles as well as the slanted cuts at the sides of the scuppers.

▲A SHINGLED KNEE WALL forms the low, curved railing on this lofty deck built at treetop level. An enclosed balustrade offers more security for high-up decks like this and also serves as a windbreak.

◀GLASS RAILING SYSTEMS are great for providing an unimpeded view and in this case, a wind-screen, but they are pricey and need to be kept clean. This type of railing style is really more of a non-style and can complement any house.

► A TRANSPARENT BALUSTRADE is created by aircraft cable stretched horizontally between steel uprights, with a wooden top rail on this raised deck. These cables are readily available at specialty hardware and stair and railing fabricators. The metal posts extend below the deck at the edge and are lag-bolted into the rim joist for stability and secure attachment.

ALTERNATIVES TO WOOD RAILINGS

There are many alternatives to wood railings, notably balustrades made up of pipe railing, wrought iron, aircraft cable, wire mesh, or glass or acrylic panels.

Painted steel or copper tubing

Galvanized steel cable

Painted steel mesh

Acrylic or glass panels

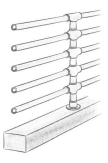

Welded steel tubing

▲THE USE OF UNUSUAL MATERIALS—like wire mesh in a wooden frame—and unexpected elements, such as the white columns, add visual interest to this deck. The rail is notched around the column for stability.

◀NAUTICAL IN FEEL, this pipe railing is well suited to its shoreline locale. Pipe railing has several advantages: It's fairly inexpensive to build, can be fabricated off-site and assembled on-site, can be painted any color, and weathers well.

▲THERE IS CRISP ARCHITECTURAL GEOMETRY at work in this contemporary railing composed of tightly spaced horizontal steel cables. The solid-wood posts are interspersed at regular intervals by thinner metal uprights, and a floorboard at each wood post running perpendicular to the rest of the decking marks the same intervals in the deck. Little details like this make a thoughtful difference in the design.

STAIRS

◄ BRIDGING TWO REGIONS of the house, this utilitarian stairway makes a straight run from a deck to a graveled patio with open risers, which are advantageous because water, leaves, and other debris can't accumulate.

► THESE CASCADING STAIRS are used to architecturally link three levels of the house, and are wide and shallow enough to linger on comfortably, creating additional subspaces and seating where guests can congregate during large parties.

Comfortable Stairs

THE BUILDING CODES governing stairs at decks are the same as for interior stairs. For utilitarian stairs descending a full story from the deck to the ground, basic dimensions of tread and riser can follow the range of maximums and minimums required by the code. But for stairs that are designed to be integrated into level changes of multiple decks, or for those that are to be more decorative or prominent, the relationship between tread and riser is more comfortable when it is not so steep. Deeper treads and shallower risers gently encourage a slower step or might offer a place to pause on a landing. For an outdoor stair, a comfortable relationship of tread to riser is a 6-in. to 7-in. riser height with a 10-in. to 12-in. tread depth. As a major traffic pathway, stairs need to be at least 3 ft. wide, but it's even better if they're 5 ft. or wider, allowing two to walk together.

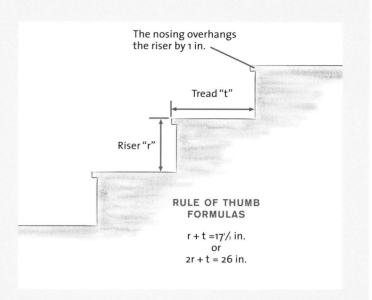

The nosing overhangs the riser by 1 in.

Tread "t"

Riser "r"

RULE OF THUMB FORMULAS

$$r + t = 17\frac{1}{2} \text{ in.}$$
or
$$2r + t = 26 \text{ in.}$$

◄ WITH ONLY THREE SHALLOW risers needed to get from the deck to the lawn, no surrounding guardrail is necessary, which means the panoramic view can be enjoyed in all its glory without interruptions.

▲ TAKING A 90-DEGREE TURN at a landing inserts a pause in ascending or descending a longer flight of stairs, and in a small area makes it easier to negotiate the change in elevation. This maze of a deck incorporates several landings—some that serve as decks themselves and others that change the direction of the stair.

▶ IN KEEPING WITH the surrounding landscape, these rustic stairs built of peeled and split logs make a perfect transition from deck to landscape.

◄ THINK OF A RAMP as an "architectural hill" rather than as a blot on the landscape, and this one blends in naturally while making it a breeze to access the deck in a wheelchair or to push a grill or stroller onto it.

Ramps

THE AMERICANS WITH DISABILITIES ACT (ADA) has made it a requirement to design new stores, apartment houses, and offices in a manner that ensures they're accessible to individuals with mobility and sensory difficulties. Although no such requirement exists for private residences, incorporating a ramp into deck design can be useful, not only for family members or guests in wheelchairs but also for wheeling grills, strollers, and other items up to a deck. Ramps are defined by their slope, a ratio between the number of inches in vertical rise per number of inches in horizontal run. The ADA requires a 1:12 slope, but for a private home, a steeper ramp (up to 1:8) also is acceptable.

◄ THE 45-DEGREE ANGLES OF THIS HOUSE are reflected in the turn of the deck's stair as it rounds the corner of the house. Changing the direction of the planking is a good idea to subtly signal a change in elevation to someone walking along.

Screens and Skirting

TRIMMING THE DECK with a skirtboard and/or a lattice screening finishes it to the same degree as the house by concealing the less elegant framing and the shadowy space beneath a raised deck.

The skirtboard runs horizontally beneath the overhanging deck boards. This can be painted to match the trim of the house's corner boards or other trim pieces, or it can match the species of the deck floor and balustrade. Either way, it should be wide enough to hide the rough framing of the deck's undercarriage.

Screening the space under the deck is generally done with closely spaced boards or a lattice, hung either diagonally or at right angles to the skirt. Covering the void helps to keep animals and debris out from under the deck. Lattice is generally bought in sections at lumberyards or home centers and can be painted or left natural. Do not let the bottom edge of the lattice touch the ground or it will get wet and begin to rot. Bordering the bottom edge of the screening with another horizontal board presents a more finished look.

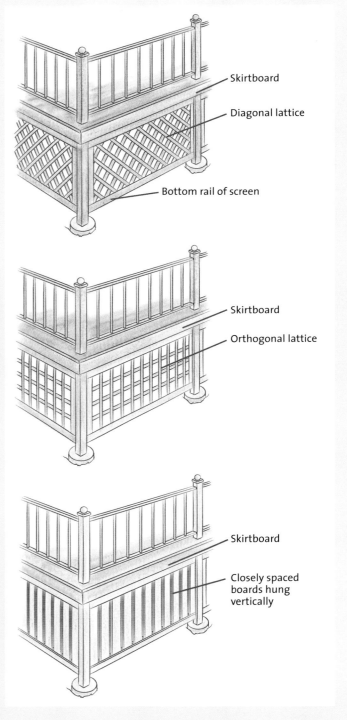

Skirtboard

Diagonal lattice

Bottom rail of screen

Skirtboard

Orthogonal lattice

Skirtboard

Closely spaced boards hung vertically

◀ THE LATTICE ON THE SIDE OF THIS DECK conceals the framing and helps keep varmints from taking up residence underneath. The same lattice is echoed in the balcony railing above.

▲ PLANTERS FORM THE GUARDRAIL on this expansive deck, which uses white lattice as screening and as a backdrop to highlight the unique twin stairs. Situating the stairs at an unusual angle to each other creates a sense of drama and sophistication that a straight stair would not.

◄ SOMETIMES MOTHER NATURE DICTATES the placement of our man-made embellishments—here the position of a beautiful, ivy-covered tree determined the location of these stairs, which were forced to jog over from the edge of the top deck. The stairs have solid risers (the vertical portion between each tread), which hide the view of the space under the upper deck and give the stair a more substantial feel.

BUILT-INS

▶ BRINGING THE CONVERSATION pit from the living room to the deck is a great idea for an outdoor room. This brick fire pit was built into a sunken deck enclosure. The semicircular built-in bench is made up of short, straight planks cut to form the curve.

◀ A COMBINATION OF BUILT-IN and freestanding furniture fills out this shady corner, giving it a real sense of enclosure, like an open-air living room. Cushions can be covered with water-repellent fabric but still shouldn't be left outside or they'll become sodden and rot. If cushions will be out all the time, they should be made of special fabrics specifically designed for outdoor use.

Built-In Benches

A BUILT-IN BENCH **is a welcome amenity to any deck. Consider the views and the function of any built-in furniture as you determine where to place a bench** and whether it should have a back or be backless. A bench placed by the door might be a convenient spot to remove muddy shoes or put down the groceries while fumbling for the keys. Built-in benches surrounding a picnic table create a permanent corner for designated dining. And long, backless benches that wrap the perimeter of a low deck are great for large gatherings, allowing guests to face the house or the view beyond.

To ensure comfortable seating, pay careful attention to the distance from the seat edge to the deck floor and from seat edge to seat back. The seat should be 15 in. to 16 in. off the floor, and the seat depth should be no less than 16 in. but no deeper than 24 in. if the bench has a back.

▲ THESE BACKLESS BUILT-IN BENCHES are designed to multitask: They define the perimeter of the low deck; they're wide enough for a sunbather to stretch out on; and they allow seating in either direction depending on the activity—taking in the view or socializing on the deck.

◄ IN THIS UNDERSTATED BUILT-IN eating area, the inset of the deck within the roof overhang makes a protected spot just outside the door. Built-in benches need to be sanded smooth periodically to avoid splinters. Note the electrical outlet—it's a waterproof type made specifically for exterior use.

◄ A CONTINUOUS BENCH ZIGZAGS around the perimeter of this angular deck. The bench is made up of the same planks as the deck floor, only turned on their sides. Slightly pitching the top surface of the guardrail helps it to shed water. The railing also conceals tiny light fixtures.

▼ ALTHOUGH THESE BENCHES ARE NOT ATTACHED to the decking, they are heavy enough to withstand high wind on this rooftop deck and are designed to fit in front of the intervals of lattice. The cushions are used seasonally and are inexpensive.

◄ THIS CIRCULAR, BUILT-IN BENCH makes a convivial and intimate spot around the fire pit at cook-out time. The colorful cushions are neatly attached with tabs so they won't shift or blow away.

Outdoor Storage

GRILL ACCESSORIES, **citronella candles, and bench cushions are most useful when kept close at hand, so it's worth designating storage for them on the deck.**

Outdoor storage needs to be easily accessible and attractive, but primarily it needs to be waterproof. A box tucked into the side of a stair landing or inside a bench is less conspicuous than a freestanding shed on a deck, but make sure the unit has a solid top to shed water and a perforated bottom to drain any water that seeps in. If you're building a new deck, storage can be incorporated into the design in the form of a built-in chest or of subdeck compartments as shown here. Consider a lockable unit for expensive accessories, hazardous items, or long-term storage.

▲ A WIRE BASKET UNDER A LID that's part of the decking is well ventilated—a clever and handy solution to storage for hoses and other outdoor tools.

Shade and Shelter

ECKS SHOULD BE ORIENTED TO GATHER AS MUCH SUN as possible, but they are most enjoyable if they provide the option of shade. Arbors, trellises, and pergolas do this while increasing the sense of shelter and security on a deck. Overhead structures also add a vertical dimension to an otherwise horizontal deck and help create a sequence of spatial experiences in our outdoor rooms, dividing and defining different areas.

Of course, positioning your deck to take advantage of natural shade can be the simplest approach, and there are other shady devices such as awnings and umbrellas that provide a less permanent solution.

▲ THE LYRICAL, ARCHED BEAMS of this picturesque arbor tie in thematically with the circles in the latticework, as well as to the arched doorway leading into the house (at right). For a little aromatherapy on the deck, choose a fragrant plant or vine, such as the wisteria used here.

▲ SURROUNDED BY WOODS, this deck on the east side of the house has great natural shade; there's partial shade by lunchtime and full shade by dinner. In the winter, there's plenty of natural light because the surrounding trees lose their leaves, warming the deck and the house naturally.

◄ THIS DECK IS ONE STEP FROM BECOMING A PORCH— you'd just have to sheath the rafters of the pergola and voila! When the overhead members of a pergola slope, they are called rafters rather than joists, as they mimic the skeletal form of a virtual roof rather than a flat ceiling. The deck edge zigzags, making each corner of it unique and offering many zones to furnish and use.

PERGOLAS, ARBORS, AND TRELLISES

▲ THE CONNECTION BETWEEN HOUSE AND GARDEN is framed by a formal overhead pergola at this shady poolside spot. The play of light and shadow creates a ribbon of virtual texture on the ground, adding another pattern to the landscaping and one that changes during the course of the day.

◄ THIS DECK ENTRANCE topped by a pergola was designed in concert with the architecture of the house and is an artful example of how a series of small spaces can be thoughtfully connected to provide an evocative transition as you move from one space to the next.

▼ HAVING DISTINCT ZONES within a commodious deck reduces the scale so it doesn't give the impression of one large platform but rather a series of areas for different uses—such as grilling, sitting, napping, or eating. A portion of this deck juts out like a stage onto the lawn, and the simple pergola acts as the proscenium defining this particular portion of the deck.

◄ A CANOPY EFFECT is created by the overhead arbor that shades this seat. Arched beams support a parade of purlins, and the entire structure is freestanding and can be moved to another spot periodically for a change in view. The teak bench structure weathers to a lovely silver gray.

▲ A PERGOLA OFFERS A SENSE of shelter but is open to the sun and stars. Here six unadorned posts support three beams that span the width of this simple structure, providing shade, intimacy, and a sense of verticality to this platform deck. The pergola also plays host to a hammock and hanging plants.

▶ THIS UNIQUE OVERHEAD structure is composed of beams reaching out from the house, with a canopy of green from the trees creating a light-filtering infill between. Clad in the same clapboard siding, the beams cleverly incorporate light fixtures for nighttime use.

Trellis, Arbor, or Pergola?

TRELLIS DESCRIBES the armature constructed from slender wooden members that are designed for plants to grow against or over. A trellis can be mounted vertically against a wall or freestanding, or can be used horizontally as the ceiling plane of an arbor.

An arbor is an outdoor room created by a freestanding three-dimensional structure made of posts and overhead joists (when they are horizontal) or rafters (when they slope). An arbor is meant to inhabit for the enjoyment of a shady spot.

A Pergola is an arbor that is attached to the house, like an open-air arcade. It provides shade on a walkway as well as shades the house's windows and glass doors from the sun's hot glare in the summer, while permitting the lower winter sun to reach the interior.

TRELLIS
In the form of a vertical lattice.

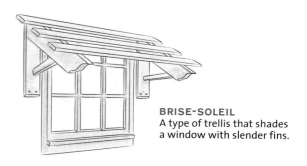

BRISE-SOLEIL
A type of trellis that shades a window with slender fins.

Interlocking joists with decorative tails

Lattice

ARBOR
An arched beam supports an overhead trellis.

Arched lattice panel

Post

PERGOLA
Interlocking joists with decorative tails

OTHER SHADY DEVICES

▲ THIS EXPANSIVE DECK MAKES WAY for nature by accommodating three large trees. The holes in the deck are large enough to allow movement, growth, and water absorption. The trees provide natural shade in the summer, while allowing solar heat to penetrate the house when they lose their leaves in the winter.

◀ WHILE THE PERGOLA ATTACHED to this house adds architectural interest and marks a transitional area between house and deck, the large umbrella provides the shade and visually anchors the deck in the landscape.

◄ A DEEP, OVERHANGING ROOF provides a welcome shadow at the edges of the house, shading the deck and the adjacent window. In the winter, when the sun angles are lower, sunlight will penetrate the house through the windows, providing natural heat.

Fabric Awnings

IN ADDITION TO PROVIDING **uninterrupted shade,** awnings can also direct rain off a deck, making them a useful alternative to open-air arbors or pergolas. Removable or retractable awnings are a good option in colder climates because they allow the sun to reach any windows off the deck in cooler months, thus maximizing heat and sunlight. There are coated fabrics made specifically for awnings, similar to those used for sunshade umbrellas; they are ideal for outdoor use but are heavy and should be fabricated by a specialist. Alternatively, thin nylon and other synthetic materials, while not as durable, can be easily sewn and attached with grommets to the substructure of a wood or metal frame.

▲ THIS DECK EMPLOYS A FABRIC AWNING that filters light and moves with the breeze, creating a fluid roof. This can be taken down after the summer and repaired and replaced easily.

5

Patios

L ike a deck, a patio allows us to take advantage of all that the great outdoors has to offer, while expanding the useful space of our abodes. Patios have evolved from mere concrete slabs into sophisticated outdoor rooms, ranging from brick courtyards to urban rooftop respites to luxurious poolside havens.

A patio can be attached to the house or placed at a distance, and can accommodate a range of activities, including dining, recreation, and quiet relaxation. Budget, lifestyle, and property dictate what type of patio will be most feasible and useful; energetic hosts might choose a large, multifaceted patio with a range of dining and seating areas, while for others, a small flagstone patch nestled in a garden would provide the perfect spot for quiet reading or reflection.

Regardless of the type of patio you choose to build, there are many architectural considerations; site, style, and materials are key. Once the basics have been decided, there are many other practical and aesthetic features to deliberate: Will steps, walls, or fences be part of the plan? Do you want any overhead structures for shade? Should there be added elements and focal points, such as fireplaces, outdoor kitchens, or water features?

◄ DYNAMIC SWIRLING PATTERNS and undulating motion are the hallmarks of this exotic courtyard patio. Paved in slate and ochre stone, it also features a blue glass mosaic that lends drama and a personalized flair to the design. The chairs and decorative railings above continue the wavy theme.

Patio Types

WITH THE ARRAY OF PAVING MATERIALS AVAILABLE, patio design can be as traditional or imaginative as you desire. But regardless of style, the majority of patios fall into one of the following categories.

An attached patio extends a house into the landscape and can be furnished like a room. A freestanding patio is generally sited to capitalize on a particular aspect of the landscape, such as a garden or a captivating view. A rooftop or balcony patio, most frequently found in urban landscapes, creates outdoor space when there's none to be had at ground level. A courtyard patio unites the wings of the house and is often designed as part of the main living space. And finally, a poolside patio focuses on recreation and entertainment. The type of patio you build should work in conjunction with your house, landscape, and lifestyle to ensure the most useful and pleasing outdoor space.

▼ THIS ATTACHED STONE PATIO is positioned to soak up the sun's radiant heat, and while the surface can be hot in the summer, it's comfortably warm in the autumn and spring, maximizing its seasonal use. Although small, the patio provides plenty of room for outdoor lounging and a pleasing transition between house and lawn.

▲ BECAUSE BALCONY AND ROOFTOP PATIOS are set well above ground level, they have some special requirements. This Spanish-style balcony patio rests atop a rounded room, so waterproofing the surface under the paving is essential. Also, the entire patio needs to slope at least ¼ in. per foot to allow water drainage.

◄ FREESTANDING PATIOS ARE A GOOD OPTION when the surrounding ground is soft or sandy, and this patio makes the most of a seaside spot, providing a seating area in the garden. Composed of gravel, which can be easily replenished as needed, the patio is lined with Belgian block edging that helps contain the gravel while adding visual interest.

▶ SURROUNDED BY A VARIETY of lush plantings, this freestanding brick patio acts as a focal point in the garden. The sundial is a traditional garden accent, but it's important to keep in mind that any accessory exposed to the elements will deteriorate quickly if it's not of good quality and designed for outdoor use.

PATIO TYPES

PATIO ON GRADE
Laid directly onto the level of the ground with no intervening steps from grass to patio. A fairly level site is required.

RAISED PATIO
Sits a few steps up from the surrounding yard and built so that one can go directly from the house onto the patio without any stairs. Also used with a sloping yard where the first floor of the house is high above the surrounding grade.

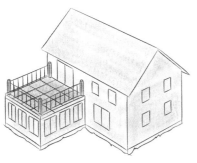

ROOFTOP PATIO
Set on top of the flat-roofed portion of a house. The roof framing of this patio must be designed to support heavy patio materials, such as concrete and stone.

POOLSIDE PATIO
The paved area immediately around a pool. Designed to withstand chlorinated water.

◀ STURDY, SQUARED-OFF COLUMNS anchor this hybrid patio and porch and support a unique overhead roof structure. Farther down the hill a freestanding patio of the same stone material is built out to face the mountains.

▼ NATURAL STONES HAVE MORE TEXTURE than cut or polished stone pavers, so wet feet won't slip as easily, making them ideal for pool patios. The large, irregular stones surrounding this poolside patio have wide spaces between them that let the grass grow through, creating a natural look that blends nicely into this rustic landscape.

▶ A COLORFUL ROOFTOP PATIO transforms what could have been a strictly utilitarian space (the stairs lead to a water tank) into an outdoor room with a view. The wider the mortar joints, the less precise you need to be about fitting irregular stones, making this type of patio a good project for do-it-yourselfers.

◀ THIS HOUSE FEATURES TWO PATIOS with very different functions; although spatially disjointed, they're visually connected by corresponding style and materials. The courtyard patio separates the garage from the house while providing a turnaround for cars, and the freestanding patio, which is cleverly sunk into an existing slope, provides a pleasant dining spot.

◄ THE NATURAL STONE FOUNDATION WALL of the house is reflected in the more refined stone that's used in the attached patio, creating a natural flow between the two. The patio further complements the house by following its contour; this design also maximizes the panoramic view.

▼ THIS STRIKING DESIGN EMPLOYS a combination of angular symmetry and contrasting curves to produce a dramatic poolside patio. The interesting color variation in the pavers prevents the layout from looking too artificial. Rougher-textured stones are used at the lip of the pool and spa for both traction and a decorative border.

Patio Materials

MATERIAL SELECTION HAS A BIG IMPACT on a patio's style. The most common patio materials are brick, stone, rock or gravel, concrete, and tile. Each has unique qualities that lend themselves to different types of designs, and they can be used in combination for added depth and texture. Brick, for instance, has an air of tradition, but it can be used in both very formal and very rustic designs. The natural beauty of stone promotes the use of regional materials to complement the local architecture. Rocks and gravel can be used loose for an informal feel, and some types can be set in mortar to create intricate mosaic patterns. Versatile, inexpensive concrete can either be poured in place or cast into varied-shape pavers that mimic other materials. Tile is particularly alluring, and although it has a rustic feel, it works well in either formal or casual settings.

In addition to pure aesthetics, when designing a patio that works for you, you'll also need to consider price, availability, and which materials can be integrated harmoniously with your house and property.

▼ MULTICOLORED CONCRETE PAVERS laid in varying patterns add dimension and flair to this refined patio. Edging the patio with multiple layers—plantings, stone wall, and wooden baluster—creates much more visual interest than a single material would.

▲ IN A DELIBERATE ATTEMPT to create an indistinct shape for this patio, slabs of limestone and strips of sod do a positive/negative dance as they weave at the margins of this deck. Limestone makes a good patio material, with edges that soften over time, creating a natural feel.

◄ THE GRAVEL "RAFT" afloat in a pond of pebbles creates a focal point in this alluring patio area. The raised platform defines a seating area within the larger space of patio and landscape. Gravel is a permeable material that allows water to soak into the earth, making it a good material in garden settings or in areas with trees nearby.

BRICK

▲ A PORCH OR DECK IS an extension of a house, but a patio is more an extension of the yard. When space permits, it's possible to create more than one patio area, as seen at this home, which has a pair of brick outdoor zones. One was placed in a sunny spot just steps down from the porch, the other in a shadier garden area at the edge of the woods.

▲ LINING THE EDGES OF PATIO STEPS accentuates them and calls attention to the change in level—an important safety feature. Here, an expansive patio is edged in railroad ties to visually break up what could otherwise be an overwhelming sea of brick. The planting bed situated between two sets of steps creates a colorful focal point.

Brick Paving

BRICK IS A COMMON MATERIAL for paving patios and walkways and comes in a huge range of colors, textures, and shapes that can be used in an infinite number of patterns. There are several kinds of brick that can be used on patios. Paving bricks are fired at very high temperatures and last longer than common brick, which is usually used for walls, though it can be used for paving in mild climates. Vintage or used brick looks nicely weathered from the beginning and blends well with plant materials. It can be mixed with granite edging or other stone pavers, as well as wood timbers.

Brick is laid either on a tamped sand base or set onto a concrete slab and mortared in place. In most paving patterns, bricks are put down with the widest face showing; the narrower sides and edges are used for borders and for special design applications. Bricks can be laid tightly together or with space between, showing grass, moss, or a wide mortar joint. Regardless, the surface can become moldy and thus slippery if it's in a damp, shady area and will have to be cleaned regularly.

▲ IN THIS COOL, SHADY SPOT topped by a rustic arbor, the brick patio is laid in a running bond pattern; the spacious fit of the bricks is forgiving when the ground heaves in colder months.

◄ THE LIVELY, HERRINGBONE pattern seen here is easy to lay once it's established at one edge or starting point. It's complemented by the more basic running bond pattern in the wall, which was kept low so as not to obstruct the view. Note the clever solution for dealing with runoff water—the downspout has an extender that removes it below the elevation of the patio.

► SETTING THIS BASKETWEAVE PATTERN in sand rather than mortar creates a more informal look. The bricks don't need to be dead level when they're set in sand, allowing for more variation in the natural topography of a site.

▼ BRICK CAN BE AN ALTERNATIVE to the ubiquitous bluestone pool patio. Bricks are visually appealing against the green grass and blue water, and they blend well with the landscaping. Chlorine stains anything, so keep that in mind when choosing materials.

BRICK PAVING PATTERNS

Running bond

Parquet or
basketweave

Herringbone

Stack bond

Sectional (like a big checkerboard)

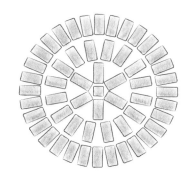

Concentric

◄ PERFECTLY SITUATED to catch the morning sun, this brick courtyard is sandwiched between the garage and the bedroom and just steps off the kitchen, making it a good place to relax with coffee and the morning paper. Like all masonry, brick retains heat, so it will warm up quickly on a chilly morning.

STONE

▲ A RADIATING STONE PATTERN punctuated by a circular planting bed with a sundial evokes a meditative path that contrasts nicely with the social seating area it connects to. The clean lines of this pattern require precise craftsmanship and a more liberal budget, but the unique result is a landscaping gem.

▲ THE NATURAL, UNCUT EDGES of these phyllite pavers (in the slate and schist family) quarried by the homeowner give the impression of free-floating islands in a gravelly sea. Casual but dramatic, the patio acts as a focal point in the landscape while still blending well with the rustic surroundings. Since the stones don't have to fit together, this free-form approach allows more leeway in stone selection and assembly.

◄ THIS CASUAL CONFIGURATION of random flagstones makes it easy to install a patio (simply set flat stones into the ground) around existing trees without disturbing their roots. The intermingling of hardscape and landscape generates an organic flow that is complemented by the overhead arbor strewn with vines.

Stone Paving

CUT STONE PAVERS, called flagstones, are large square or rectangular stones, about 2 in. thick, with smooth faces and square edges, although irregular-shaped flagstones are also available. Pavers can be laid in ordered rows or in more random patterns. The types of stone most often used for flagstone are slate, bluestone, and sandstone. Fieldstone and other rough stones look the most natural, but they are uneven in thickness and need to be set carefully to achieve a level patio.

Another type of stone used for paving is stone blocks, or cobbles; these are made of granite and referred to as Belgian block. Because of its uneven surface and expense, Belgian block is most often used in small areas or for edging another material, such as granite, brick, or flagstone.

▲ A SEA OF STONE BLOCKS CAN LOOK MONOLITHIC, but the added pattern of the larger pavers breaks up the expanse on this formal patio. The pathways implied by the block areas lead to a shady place under the arbor.

◄ THE OVERALL DIMENSIONS of this compact patio match the scale and proportions of the adjacent portion of the house, making a cohesive whole of outdoor and indoor spaces. The pavers laid in a neat grid pattern contrast nicely with the more random look of the old stone house.

▲ STONE PAVERS HAVE TO BE MEASURED precisely in an elegant setting like this one, where a clear, curved line is drawn between patio and manicured lawn. On a large patio that is set in mortar, there needs to be a slight slope so that water can run off toward the grass.

► USING REGIONAL MATERIALS for paving and planting creates a naturally harmonious effect. Here, large limestone pavers form a patio that meanders through planting beds, and different-height blocks of the same stone add a vertical dimension. Space has been left between the blocks for plants to thrive.

STONE PAVING PATTERNS

Random with cut pavers

Random with irregular pavers

Regular rows with cut pavers
of equal size

Regular rows with cut pavers
of varying sizes

▼ ALTERNATING WIDTHS in the running bond pattern of these bluestone pavers gives a sense of movement to this patio, which winds between the house and shed. Planting beds placed where stone pavers were omitted at the perimeter offers gardeners an accessible bed and brings the plants tableside. When installing your patio, remember to plan for long-term growth in the plantings or use annuals.

Code Considerations

ALTHOUGH PATIOS GENERALLY aren't covered by building codes, they may be subject to local zoning codes, which vary by municipality. For instance, towns that limit the total area of developed land surface on a given property may consider the square footage of a patio the same as a building's square footage; others don't count patios at all. In addition, the setback requirements for buildings may also extend to setback requirements for patios, limiting the proximity of your patio to your property line. Knowing what the parameters are for your property before you plan a patio can save you a lot of time, money, and frustration if you end up finding out the hard way.

▲ PATIOS LAID WITH CLOSELY FITTED STONES like this need to be pitched slightly to allow rainwater to run off. The irregularly shaped stones are fitted together in a gentle arc to form a gracious patio that extends along the front of the house. With distinct zones at either end, there's plenty of room for different activities here.

◄ A "BARELY THERE" PATIO like this can evolve and expand over time as you collect rocks from the outer landscape and bring them home. Conforming to the gentle slope of the lawn, this charming patio has the appearance of a naturally occurring rock formation.

ROCK AND GRAVEL

▲ THIS SCULPTURE GARDEN features a stone patio with a seating area abutting a gravel wraparound, which extends the patio area and forms a meditative path. Although the stone patio is permanent, the planter boxes and gravel can be reconfigured or expanded fairly easily if so desired, offering flexibility to this outdoor space.

◄ WHIMSICAL PATIOS WITH DETAILED PATTERNS can be created simply by setting small pebbles in mortar. Here, contrasting colors of the same material show off the craftsman's talent and delicate design sense. While beautiful and unique, pebble mosaics can be labor-intensive and thus expensive; using them solely for accents can cut down on costs.

▲ GRAVEL OR PEA STONE PROVIDES a less formal patio, which can be easily expanded at any time with a truckload of additional stones. Although it's difficult to walk barefoot on gravel, it drains well when it rains or snows.

Paving with Rock and Gravel

GRAVEL, FROM WHITE MARBLE CHIPS to ordinary gray pea stones, is a relatively cheap, locally obtainable patio material. Round, tumbled stone gravel is kinder to bare feet than crushed stone, which can have sharp edges. Organic material, such as grass or weeds, should be removed before laying a gravel bed—a depth of 6 in. to 8 in. is ideal. Some type of edging, which can be anything from stone to wood to brick, is needed to contain the bed. Gravel patios are fairly easy to maintain by raking regularly and replenishing annually. They drain well, though they're difficult to shovel in snowy climates.

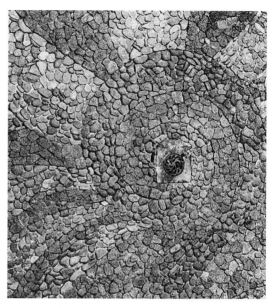

◄▲ RIVER ROCKS ARE LARGE PEBBLES worn smooth by water over many years, and those used for this mosaic-style patio were locally quarried. The swirling petal patterns created by the colorful rocks set in mortar lend a sense of artistic formality to this sophisticated outdoor room.

► THIS STRIKING PATIO features pavers cut on a curve and laced with gravel, which provides far more design flexibility than mortar would. Distinct geometric shapes like this circle demonstrate how a graphic design pattern can be used in paving to direct a gaze, create a focal point, or define a zone in a larger context.

CONCRETE

▲ THIS CURVY PATIO EXEMPLIFIES the versatility of concrete. Tinted a warm brown color, the concrete was poured into curved forms and was then stamped with an irregular geometric pattern that mimics stone pavers.

◀ SMALL CONCRETE PAVERS contrast with the broad and tall concrete wall on this patio, while the streaming horizontal vine adds dimension and a dramatic splash of color. Large expanses of concrete may need control joints or expansion joints to direct any cracking as the material shrinks and expands; this holds true for both horizontal slabs and vertical walls.

Concrete Paving

MANUFACTURED CONCRETE PAVERS are extremely durable and replicate the look of natural stone (or brick) but are more regular in size and shape and less expensive. They can be laid randomly or in patterns similar to brick patterns. Some manufacturers offer concrete pavers with interlocking shapes.

Concrete can also be poured in place within borders of stone, wood, or brick. Slab-formed concrete is quite versatile: It can be heavily textured with an aggregate of stone; it can be scored, brushed, or pigmented during installation for additional texture and color; it can be stamped with a pattern when wet to resemble paving patterns of other materials; or it can be embedded with other elements, such as small pebbles or glass, for accents.

▲ A COURTYARD OF RADIATING CONCRETE PAVERS is formed within the two wings of this grand, hillside home. Built-in brick planters define the edge of the courtyard, while offering an alluring contrast in material.

◄ AN UNEXPECTED AND PRIVATE PATIO in a small lot is a pleasant alternative to a limited lawn. Here, stone steps lead down to a sunny patio set in a parquet pattern of concrete pavers that is screened from neighbors by a substantial trellis.

TILE

◄ SANDWICHED BETWEEN the pool and the lake, this tile patio presents a serene plateau. Commercial-grade tiles are particularly durable for poolside patios that get a lot of use.

▼ UNGLAZED QUARRY TILES such as these are made specifically for outdoor use and are ideal for pool surrounds. The tiles are set on a concrete base and then mortared in place. The grid of the patio tiles here is set at an intriguing angle, and the square tiles echo the window pattern of the house.

TERRACING TECHNIQUES

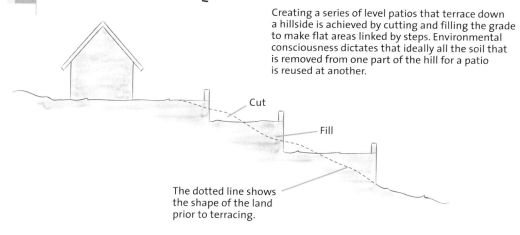

Creating a series of level patios that terrace down a hillside is achieved by cutting and filling the grade to make flat areas linked by steps. Environmental consciousness dictates that ideally all the soil that is removed from one part of the hill for a patio is reused at another.

Cut

Fill

The dotted line shows the shape of the land prior to terracing.

▲ WHEN A HOUSE HAS ACCESS to its outdoor rooms from many different levels and the property is sloped, terracing is a good way to optimize quirky space. At this multilevel patio, the bridge offers an intriguing alternative to stairs as a way of entering the house (far right) and underscores the trail to take up the hill to another outdoor zone.

TO LIFE BOATS.

6

Cooking and Dining

Family and friends have gathered in the kitchen for years—not just to eat but also to catch up on the day's activities and socialize. With the growing interest in casual outdoor entertaining, it's natural for such gatherings to shift to backyard cooking areas.

Enhanced grill features, innovative entertainment islands, and self-sufficient outdoor kitchens have made cooking and dining alfresco easier than ever before, whether it's tossing a few burgers on the grill or creating a gourmet meal from scratch. Although you can get by with a portable grill for basic backyard barbecues, investing in a permanent outdoor cooking center can simplify food preparation and serving, while also accommodating more elaborate affairs. These units can include multiple cooking surfaces, extended counter space, under-counter refrigerators, and bar sinks, all of which make outdoor dining (and cleanup) easier and more enjoyable.

Equally important as cooking areas are eating areas. Comfortable, stylish furnishings have made it a pleasure to relax and dine in the sun or beneath a starry sky. From chic bistro tables to grilling islands with bar seating to classic teak dining sets with expandable seating, weather-resistant furniture is available to suit nearly every decorating style and gathering size.

◄ CONVENIENTLY LOCATED just beyond the kitchen door, this dining nook offers a comfortable place to gather for meals that have been prepared in the kitchen or on the grill. The low hedge, cut-stone paving, and vine-covered arbor create the sense of an outdoor room.

▲ WEATHER CONDITIONS are always a consideration when planning an outdoor cooking and dining area. The tall hedge and house wall screen this grill from breezes, and the umbrella can be raised or lowered throughout the season depending on the sun's intensity.

▶ PLACING THIS GRILL along the outer edge of the patio helps define the space and frees up the patio itself for dining, entertaining, or other activities. It also keeps the heat away from activity areas.

▲ TWO SEPARATE DINING AREAS make this space adaptable. Counter seating, under the pergola, is convenient for snacks, conversing with the chef, and quick weeknight dinners. The dining area nearby is preferred for more leisurely sit-down dinners and larger gatherings with friends.

Choosing a Location

COOKING AND DINING AREAS created on decks, patios, porticos, or porches offer convenience to kitchens and baths and make it easy to access gas, water, and power for grills or cooking centers. Their proximity to the house also tends to encourage frequent use.

However, cooking and dining areas located away from the house can offer a greater sense of outdoor living and may capitalize on special views or serve as gathering places around pools or gardens. Because they are located farther from the house, these areas should be designed with greater self-sufficiency in mind. Additional amenities and storage may need to be installed or constructed, and professionals may need to be hired for involved projects, like wiring.

▲ THIS OUTDOOR KITCHEN is protected
from the elements by a portico but
requires a grill hood to vent away
smoke. The kitchen also features a
prep sink, under-counter refrigerator,
and storage cabinets. Tile countertops
and a tile backsplash give the kitchen
character.

▶ THE PATTERNED FLOOR AND BEAMED
CEILING define this outdoor dining
room, situated just steps away from
the sheltered outdoor kitchen and
hearth. The cabinet above the hearth
houses a television, making this seating area a favorite gathering spot on
game night.

◄ THIS INNOVATIVE DINING AND FOOD PREPARATION AREA was created with inexpensive materials. The snack bar was built from recycled roofing metal and an old sink while the chairs were rescued from a flea market. The table and countertops display tile mosaics laid in concrete by the homeowner.

Bringing in the Pros

CONSTRUCTING AN OUTDOOR KITCHEN can be a lot like building or remodeling an indoor kitchen. Chances are you'll need access to water, power, and gas lines. If you're installing a grill, the housing unit and adjacent cabinetry must meet fire-safety standards. And all sinks, refrigerators, and ice makers require adequate waste-water drainage.

The more complex the project, the more a design professional can help simplify the process. A kitchen designer, landscape architect, or general contractor can help you make the most of available space, sort out design options, plan for utilities, locate construction materials, acquire any appropriate building permits, and oversee installation.

▲ POSITIONED ALONG THE EDGE of the backyard to take advantage of a view of California's Simi Valley, this outdoor kitchen is an inviting backyard destination. An open railing behind the kitchen retains views while ensuring safety on the steep site.

Grills

FOOD SIMPLY TASTES BETTER when it's cooked outdoors. Whether it's the fresh air, searing coals, or relaxed atmosphere that makes the difference, grilling ranks among today's hottest outdoor activities. In response to this growing market, manufacturers have introduced grills in every price range and with an expanded array of features, such as multiple fuel options, assorted configurations, and innovative new accessories.

Homeowners can choose from portable, pedestal, cabinet, drop-in, or site-built grills and fire them up with wood, charcoal, propane, natural gas, electricity, or infrared heat. These grills can be customized to suit cooking preferences with adjustable fire pans, side burners, smoker boxes, rotisseries, woks, warming ovens, deep fryers, griddles, and searing grids. This array of high-tech options, along with built-in temperature gauges, long-handled utensils, grilling baskets, specialty cookbooks, and, of course, just the right apron, can turn novice and experienced cooks into grilling enthusiasts in no time.

▼ MULTIPLE GRILLING RACKS on this site-built charcoal barbecue allow foods to be cooked over hot or warm coals. A nearby egg-shaped kamado cooker is used for smoking meats. Charcoal, a charcoal-chimney starter, and grilling supplies are stored in a cabinet beneath the granite countertop.

◄ TASK LIGHTING is an important addition near grills where ambient light falls off sharply after dark. Here, a lamp was mounted in the stucco-and-tile wall above the grill. A second task lamp was added near the corner sink.

▲ THE STAINLESS-STEEL CABINET DOORS beneath this grill provide access to the inner workings of the natural-gas grill. (On a propane grill, the tanks would be located here.) This space is also used for storing tools such as a grill thermometer and wire brush.

▶ THIS PROFESSIONAL-GRADE, stainless-steel, eight-burner gas grill was designed to feed a crowd. Ample Btu and a large cooking surface make it easy to keep up with the demands of a large gathering. The butcher-block island on casters can be moved about as needed.

▼ THIS MEDIUM-SIZED GAS GRILL is perfect for family dinners and features an additional burner useful for preparing side dishes. Gas grills are a smart choice for those who grill on weeknights because they heat up quickly and require minimal attention.

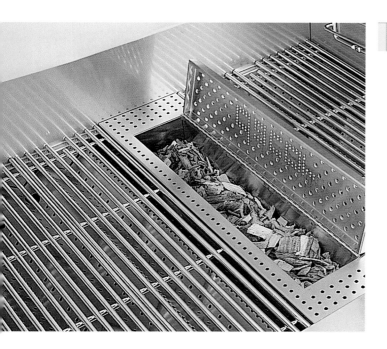

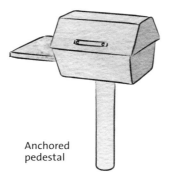 SMOKER BOXES are now available on many gas grills. Wood chips, such as mesquite, apple, or hickory, are soaked in water and placed in the smoker boxes (or in foil packets placed on the grate). The steaming chips flavor the meat during a slow-cooking process.

Smart Shopping

IT'S EASY TO GET SIDETRACKED by all the bells and whistles when shopping for a grill. The most important things to consider are how large a grilling surface you need and what type of fuel you prefer. Carry along a list of desired features and know how you will use your grill: nightly or just occasionally, for small gatherings or large parties, year-round or just in the summer. Also, look for these features:

- Sturdy construction
- Built-in thermometer—not essential, but convenient
- Rust-proof grill racks
- Easy-to-remove ash or drip pans
- At least two heat zones on a gas grill
- Adjustable vents on the top and bottom of charcoal grills

GRILL STYLES

Fire pit

Freestanding portable

Anchored pedestal

Rolling cart

Kamado cooker

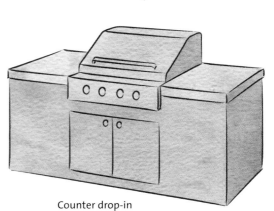

Counter drop-in

▲ ROTISSERIE ATTACHMENTS FOR GRILLS can be used for roasting whole birds or large cuts of meat. They rotate for slow, even cooking. Some gas grills feature an infrared rotisserie burner, which provides very hot, concentrated heat to speed the cooking process.

► JUST ABOUT ANYTHING that can be cooked in a conventional oven can be cooked in a wood-fired oven, but pizzas and breads are the most popular. This clay, wood-burning oven was hand-crafted by the owners, who were inspired by Asian design. Prefabricated ovens and professionally built ovens are also available.

A Simple Barbecue Pit

OLD-FASHIONED BARBECUE PITS, **like those still found in many campgrounds, offer an easy, affordable, and nostalgic method of backyard grilling over wood or coals. They can be built with concrete blocks, bricks, or stone, with stationary or adjustable grill racks. The building materials for these grills may be dry-stacked for temporary use or mortared for greater permanence. As an alternative to a grill rack, it is also possible to grill over a fire using wire baskets, long-handled skewers, or a mesh screen laid over the firebox. Just be sure to use hot pads so you don't get burned, and keep a safe distance from any flames.**

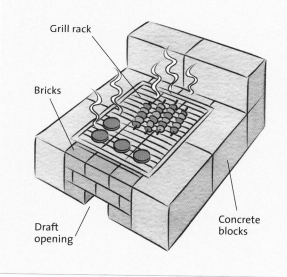

Grill rack

Bricks

Draft opening

Concrete blocks

◄ ONE OR MORE SIDE BURNERS, which can be used with or without the grill, are handy for simmering sauces, boiling corn or lobster, sautéing vegetables, or steaming side dishes. They can also keep meats warm as they come off the grill.

► THIS KAMADO-STYLE COOKER, which was designed to burn hardwood charcoal, can be used for either grilling or smoking. Its compact size is more appropriate for small gatherings and makes it ideal for tight spaces such as this condominium courtyard.

▲ THE SMALL SECTION OF THIS CHARCOAL GRILL is used when cooking just for two, while both sections can be fired up when serving a crowd. An all-day fire can also be maintained in the small unit, allowing meats to be smoked slowly in the larger section.

Cooking Centers

COOKING CENTERS ARE THE NEXT STEP beyond the grill itself. They may be simple cabinets built around drop-in charcoal or gas grills for food preparation and serving, or fully equipped outdoor kitchens with generous counters, storage cabinets, prep sinks, under-counter refrigerators, ice makers, and other outdoor-grade appliances.

On a smaller scale, a bar or entertainment island is an affordable and practical accompaniment to a freestanding grill. Many of these units come with wheels so that they can be easily repositioned depending on the occasion. In many instances, cabinets with countertops can be built around existing grills. When choosing materials, keep in mind the cooking area's location. Beneath the cover of a porch or portico, outdoor kitchens can feature interior-grade materials, but if exposed to the elements, they should be constructed with durable, all-weather materials.

▼ A REFRIGERATOR makes this grilling station more functional. In addition to storing cold drinks, it's a convenient place to stash afternoon snacks and sandwich ingredients. Extra meat can be kept cool until tossed on the grill, and salads can be kept fresh until serving time.

◄ BY ADDING SEVERAL SHORT COUNTER-TOPS near the bar sink, the homeowners can separate food and beverage preparation from the serving area. The broad, curving counter can be used for serving a meal buffet style or adapted for dining with the addition of stools.

Battle of the BTU

S INCE BRITISH THERMAL UNITS (BTU) vary from one grill to another and are often hyped in sales literature to make a grill sound more powerful, it's natural to think that more is better. Although Btu reflect the heat output of the burners, they are more closely related to fuel consumption than to how hot a grill gets; this is due to the fact that grill size, construction materials, and overall design also affect the heat level. As a rule of thumb, plan on 100 Btu per sq. in. of grill space. A 300-sq.-in. grill needs approximately 30,000 Btu to operate efficiently. Higher Btu may simply waste fuel or be a sign of inefficient design.

► THIS SMALL PREP SINK, sheltered beneath a portico, is ideal for scrubbing vegetables and washing hands. It is also convenient for rinsing dirty dishes before carrying them to the kitchen. In a pinch, the sink can be filled with ice to chill canned drinks.

◀ NONFLAMMABLE, WATER-RESISTANT MATERIALS, such as the stone and stucco used here, are preferable for outdoor cabinets. Concrete block with brick or tile veneer is also an excellent choice. Provided a metal fire shield is constructed around the grill, rot-resistant wood cabinets may be used as well.

▶ THIS COOKING CENTER makes the most of minimal space. The raised counter extension allows for both grilling and pull-up seating on a single cabinet base. And building the posts into the counter was also a space-saving adaptation.

Anatomy of an Outdoor Kitchen

AN OUTDOOR KITCHEN CONTAINS **many, but not usually all, of the same elements as an indoor kitchen. Dishwashers, for instance, are not as common outdoors because dishes are often washed and stored inside the house for sanitary reasons. Also, omitting the dishwasher eliminates the need to run hot-water lines to the outdoor kitchen.**

Sinks, adequate lighting, and ample counter space rate high both indoors and out. At least some storage space is generally considered essential outdoors, especially if the kitchen is located a long way from the house. Refrigerators and ice makers, while not essential, are popular outdoor appliances that make entertaining easier.

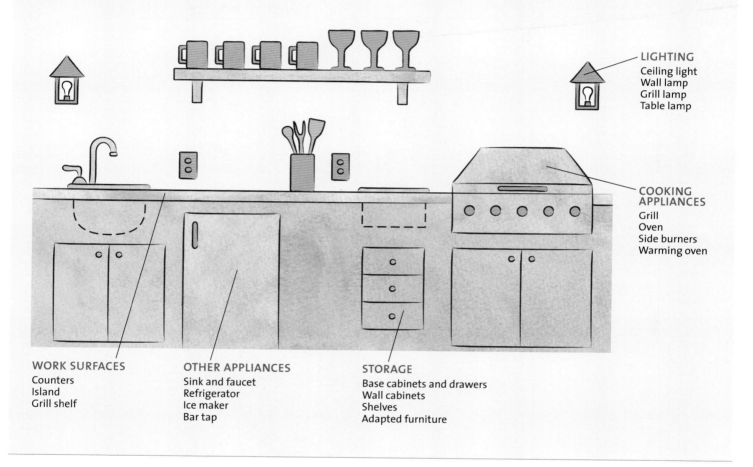

LIGHTING
Ceiling light
Wall lamp
Grill lamp
Table lamp

COOKING APPLIANCES
Grill
Oven
Side burners
Warming oven

WORK SURFACES
Counters
Island
Grill shelf

OTHER APPLIANCES
Sink and faucet
Refrigerator
Ice maker
Bar tap

STORAGE
Base cabinets and drawers
Wall cabinets
Shelves
Adapted furniture

◄ FUNCTIONALITY IS A HALLMARK of this triangular work space, which occupies one corner of a square patio. It features several expanses of tile countertops for food preparation and serving, as well as plenty of under-counter bays for a trash receptacle, recyclables, and storage.

▶ A KITCHEN COUNTER WITH A SINK and under-counter refrigerator was built on the back of this stairwell that leads from an upper deck. As a space-saving convenience, a portable grill is kept in the closet, where it can be rolled out when needed.

▼ THESE HOMEOWNERS ALREADY HAD A PORTABLE GRILL, so they simply built a cabinet with generous counters and storage space around it. When the time comes, they can lift the grill out of the opening and drop in a new one.

Counter Configurations

There are at least as many **counter configurations** for outdoor kitchens as there are for indoor kitchens. One cook may want to do little more than grill meat. Another may want to have all the amenities of an indoor kitchen, plus a wood-burning pizza oven. Some prefer areas dedicated solely to cooking, while others use counters for food preparation, cooking, eating, and entertaining.

A traditional work triangle created with a sink, grill, and refrigerator is as efficient outdoors as it is indoors, but it's not essential. The key is designing something that suits a particular style of cooking and entertaining. There are many options, including single counters and galley arrangements, as well as curved, triangular, L-shaped, and U-shaped configurations.

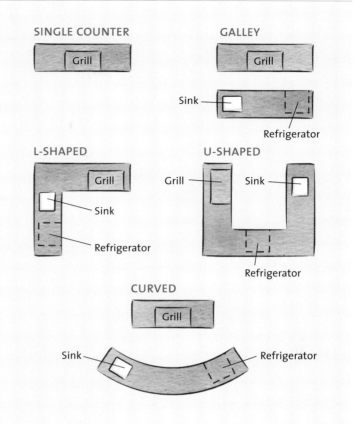

► THE FAUCET ON THIS OLD CERAMIC SINK is hooked up to waterlines in the adjacent building. By placing an outdoor sink near a building, construction costs can be kept to a minimum because existing utility lines can be tapped into easily.

▲ THIS PREFABRICATED GRILL CABINET features a countertop that extends in a circular fashion on one end to accommodate pull-up seating for two beneath a built-in shade umbrella. It sits on a stucco and faux-stone-veneer cabinet base.

▶ THIS GRILL, REFRIGERATOR, AND FOOD PREPARATION AREA was recessed into an exterior wall. The owners chose to match the veneer of the hood vent to the surroundings so that a fireplace on an adjacent wall would remain the primary focal point of the pavilion.

Choosing a Countertop

WHEN CHOOSING OUTDOOR COUNTERTOPS, **durability is as important as good looks.** The most durable and elegant choices include granite and marble, which are stain resistant, water resistant, and cool to the touch even in direct sunlight. Glazed tile, while not quite as durable or natural looking as granite or marble, offers many of the same benefits at a fraction of the cost and with far greater variety in color, pattern, and texture.

Many additional materials can be used outdoors but require more care or careful use. Artificial stone countertops are often a good option, but their ability to withstand the weather may vary, so check with the manufacturer before placing an order. Unglazed tiles, as well as bluestone, flagstone, and slate, can be beautiful and rugged—provided they are sealed for stain resistance, easier cleaning, and to help prevent the spread of germs. Stainless steel is a possibility for shaded areas, but it will heat up quickly if placed in direct sunlight; it can also scratch. And when exposed to salt spray from the ocean, stainless steel has a tendency to rust.

Laminate countertops should be avoided outdoors, as they will quickly deteriorate when exposed to sun, rain, and freezing temperatures. Wood should also be avoided; it is flammable, does not weather the elements well, and is hard to keep sanitary in outdoor conditions.

▲ THE POLISHED GRANITE COUNTERTOP on this stainless-steel cabinet withstands an outdoor setting well. It is easy to clean, provides a smooth working surface, is heat and stain resistant, and is durable even in cold climates because it is porous and thus won't crack when frozen.

◄ THIS OUTDOOR KITCHEN is used primarily for grilling and additional storage. The traditional indoor cabinetry matches the cabinets in the adjacent kitchen (viewed through the windows). The portico provides plenty of shelter to protect the wood finishes, and the entire area has been screened in.

Alfresco Dining

WHETHER COOKING INDOORS OR OUT, it's refreshing to dine alfresco. On cool days, a sunny spot is ideal. In hot weather, something shaded may be more suitable. A market umbrella or retractable awning can be opened or closed as conditions change, and a vine-covered arbor provides increased shade as the season warms up.

Before purchasing furniture, give some thought to how it will be used. A bistro table may be ideal for a light lunch or romantic dinner for two, but it won't accommodate a growing family for dinner. A dining table with optional leaves can be easily adjusted if gatherings vary in size, and a buffet-style serving area is an excellent option when entertaining a crowd. And for space-saving convenience, a cooking island can double as a bar with stools. Also consider the style and materials of furnishings, as they vary in weight, durability, and ease of care.

► THIS COZY PATIO IS JUST THE RIGHT SIZE for a small family or two couples to share a sunset dinner. Although it is open to views and a ceiling of sky, the low wall helps define the space and create a sense of enclosure.

▼ THE TALL BACKS AND SIMPLE LINES on these teak chairs add visual weight and create an atmosphere of understated elegance on this low deck, where the view is clearly the main attraction. High-backed chairs provide better support and greater comfort when sitting for long periods.

► DINING AREAS DESIGNED AS DESTINA-
TIONS, like this nook in a sandy dune,
can turn dinner into an outdoor adventure. The key to success is advanced
planning—the lighter the load and the
fewer trips made back and forth to
the house, the better.

◀ TEAK IS THE MOST WIDELY ADAPTABLE of all outdoor furniture materials. It is sturdy and rot resistant, and it weathers beautifully to a tawny gray. It is equally at home in a formal landscape or in a more relaxed setting, as illustrated here.

▲ WITH A LITTLE IMAGINATION, dining outdoors can make you feel years younger. This casual setting—a cozy space enclosed by lush foliage and a soft carpet of mulch—calls to mind secret gardens and childhood tea parties.

◀ THE FURNITURE, DINNERWARE, GARDEN STRUCTURES, containers, and plantings work in unison to carry out a sophisticated Asian style and lush green color scheme in this outdoor dining room. Food and soothing music from the outdoor sound system will add the finishing touches for a dinner party.

Creating a Cozy Space

THE MOST INVITING DINING AREAS are cozy and convey a sense of intimacy. On urban lots, that can often be achieved by providing screening between houses. Trees and mixed plantings make an effective natural buffer, while strategically placed wood fences or masonry walls can screen unwanted views and create a sense of enclosure. If neighboring houses are two-story structures, consider adding an arbor over the dining area for additional screening.

On large or open lots, it may be more effective to enclose only the dining area, leaving glimpses of the yard or garden beyond while still creating a roomlike atmosphere. Walls and fences can be covered with vines, espaliered trees, wall planters, fountains, mirrors, and other decorative objects to create a space with personality. Likewise, on a large deck or patio, a cluster of planted containers can help define a smaller, cozier area specifically for dining.

▲ EVEN THOUGH THIS FOUR-PERSON TABLE sits out in the lawn, a cozy dining area has been created by constructing a tall, wooden privacy fence and by planting a dense screen of shrubs, ornamental grasses, and flowering perennials.

► THIS FESTIVE TIKI HUT is the hub of backyard activities. Located in southern Florida, where it is blistering hot much of the year, the shade and ceiling fan are much appreciated. The bar is a casual gathering spot as well as a place to dine.

▲ ALTHOUGH IT IS A CONTINUATION of the broader deck, this dining area is clearly defined by its placement on a lower level. The different levels help to visually connect the house with the landscape, making the gathering area a central point of focus.

◄ THIS HOMEOWNER MADE HIS OWN DINING TABLE from objects one might expect to find around the garden—an oversized ceramic planter and a round-cut stone. Such elements help the seating area look comfortably at home against the backdrop of a soothing foliage garden.

◄ A RUGLIKE PATTERN of stone paving beneath this iron-and-glass dinner set creates a colorful, roomlike atmosphere. Similar effects can be achieved with brick patterns, stone and tile mosaics, and decorative concrete stains.

▼ THIS PICNIC TABLE is advantageously positioned between the lawn and a lush garden to create a cozy setting. The paving defines the patio, and container plantings are strategically positioned to clearly mark the passageways between the spaces.

◄ THIS OUTDOOR ROOM PROVIDES a casual eating area, making use of versatile, space-saving side tables rather than one large dining table. The space is clearly defined by the arbor, boulder garden, and broadened area laid in mortared stone.

▼ THESE HOMEOWNERS BUILT A DECK to make the most of their steep lot, and in doing so, they created a magical dining area that is, literally, in the treetops. The blue paint and accent items reinforce the impression of being near the sky.

▲ EVEN WHEN SPACE IS TIGHT, as it is on this deck, it is important to provide passages 3 ft. to 4 ft. wide for traffic flow. As a rule of thumb, allow at least 8 ft. square for a table that seats four.

Recycled Ideas

RECYCLED BUILDING MATERIALS look right at home outdoors, and using them reduces the amount of waste sent to landfills. Special finds from the local salvage yard or flea market can also give instant personality and character to an outdoor room. Consider these possibilities:

- Old bricks give patio floors a lived-in look.
- Worn-out chandeliers easily convert for candlelight.
- Pots and jars shine as candleholders or flower vases.
- Old sinks enhance an outdoor kitchen.
- Broken dishes and tiles enliven countertops when laid in mosaic patterns.
- Old signs are eye-catching mounted on entertainment islands.
- Metal pails filled with ice are perfect for serving chilled drinks at parties.

▲ EATING IN THE GARDEN is a celebration of where food comes from. This shaded dining table is surrounded by a series of raised-bed gardens featuring vegetables, herbs, and flowers. The crushed gravel creates a casual patio setting and drains quickly after a rain.

▲ CANDLELIGHT TRANSFORMS THIS TROPICAL GARDEN SETTING into a romantic one once the sun goes down. In addition to candleholders on the table, lanterns with candles have been hung on low posts around the perimeter of the stone patio for ambience as well as safety.

◄ THIS COOKING AND DINING AREA is located beneath a vine-covered arbor, anchored by bold columns that match those on the house. It is a large area conducive to entertaining and doubles as a passageway to the swimming pool and putting green below.

Mosquito Control

With the increased spread of mosquito-borne viruses, bug control is a growing concern for many homeowners. The best defense against mosquitoes is eliminating any standing water where they might breed. In ponds, add moving water or introduce fish to eat the larvae; mosquito tablets may also help.

Spray yourself with bug repellent, especially if you're exposed to mosquitoes for a prolonged period. And if that isn't enough, place a container of geranium oil repellent on a table, or spread an organic powder repellent on your lawn. Mechanical options for control include fuel-powered mosquito traps that attract and catch blood-seeking insects such as mosquitoes, no-see-ums, and sand gnats.

▲ EVEN CITY DWELLERS can have a private outdoor dining retreat. What might have been wasted space beneath a staircase is cleverly utilized to create a cozy, shaded dining spot for two. It is surrounded and softened by lush greenery and brightened by colorfully painted columns.

▲ THE WOODEN ARBOR DEFINES the ceiling and corners of this outdoor room, which is used for both grilling and eating. The grill is located in the far corner, away from the eating counter, to minimize the effect of the heat and smoke it generates.

7

Relaxing and Escaping

With today's fast pace of living, everyone needs a place to relax—somewhere to simply be and not do. No place is better suited for unwinding than home, but it helps to designate a space away from the telephone, television, home office, laundry room, and other activity areas.

Whether it's a screened porch, rooftop oasis, garden getaway, or backyard spa, a well-designed retreat incorporates the elements that its users find most relaxing. For some, that means a comfortable chair surrounded by lush foliage and soft music. Others may prefer a rocking chair on a balcony or a float drifting in the pool. Regardless, soothing colors, natural textures, soft light, and the sounds of chirping birds, trickling fountains, or whirring ceiling fans are all good bets for lowering your blood pressure.

Spaces in which to stretch out and nap—a sleeping porch, hammock, or sofa with a light throw—are especially appealing. However, some people find that escaping the stresses of daily life is best achieved by being active in a relaxing way. Backyard workshops, studios, and greenhouses are ideal for such pursuits. Lounging around an outdoor hearth, soaking in a therapeutic spa, or showering au natural can also do the trick.

◀ THIS PORCH STRIKES A BALANCE between the architectural formality of the house and a comfortable outdoor setting. Architectural elements with exterior exposures are stained white to match the house trim. The rafter ceiling, timber mantel, and stone-veneered fireplace introduce natural materials.

Screened Porches and Sunrooms

SCREENED PORCHES ALLOW YOU TO EXPERIENCE the fresh air, cool breezes, and soothing sounds of nature while offering protection from the summer sun, seasonal rains, and pesky insects. A 300-sq.-ft. to 400-sq.-ft. porch offers ample space for relaxing and dining, and a rectangular floor plan offers greater design flexibility than a square one. When a porch is added to an existing house, it's important for it to blend in with the architecture. Painting or staining the wood to match the house or trim color, as well as adding architectural details used in the house, will create a sense of unity.

Similar in size and location to screened porches, sunrooms are light-filled spaces that can be enjoyed year-round. Surrounded by glass, they extend visually into the landscape yet may be heated or cooled for comfort. They are excellent places to grow houseplants, host a small luncheon, or curl up with a good book.

◀ LOCATED WELL ABOVE THE TREETOPS, this upper-level porch offers excellent views of the coast. High ceilings add to the spacious atmosphere but still offer shelter from the rain and sun. Screened walls allow gentle breezes to pass through, while helping to moderate wind gusts.

▶ THIS VACATION HOME IN THE BLUE RIDGE MOUNTAINS is half porch, half deck, providing the owners with multiple spaces for outdoor living. A broad front porch and rear deck flank a generous screened porch with a stacked-stone fireplace for relaxing outdoors even on chilly days.

◄ THE DOOR LEADING FROM THIS PORCH to the outside stoop is cleverly designed to match the broad, screened wall panels; only the door handle and automatic-closing device give it away. The porch trim is painted forest green to match the house and deck trim.

Designing Porch Walls

To MAXIMIZE THE OUTDOOR ATMOSPHERE, screen porch walls from floor to ceiling. For a roomlike setting, enclose the lower section with bead board or other siding. As an alternative, sandwich the screen between decorative trim to create a semi-enclosed lower wall with architectural character.

▲ NOT ALL PORCHES HAVE WOOD FLOORS, although additional structural support may be required for stone, brick, or tile floors. The mortared flagstone on this porch adds visual warmth and character, and it also ties the room to the surrounding landscape.

◄ SINCE ALL OF THE JOINTS in a porch are exposed rather than hidden behind walls, precision construction is important. This porch features many finely executed curved details—rounded corner brackets, rafter tips, and cap rails atop the solid wall.

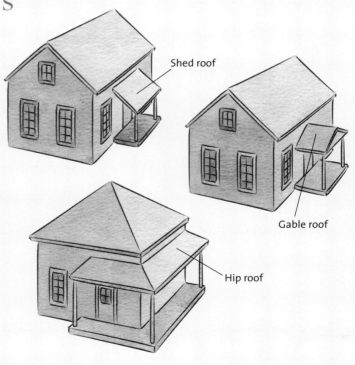

◄ THIS DECK WAS DESIGNED as a quiet retreat in the treetops. The simplicity of furnishings helps create a contemplative environment for reading or a nap, and the clean lines of the building materials visually connect this space to the house.

Protective Porch Roofs

PORCH ROOFS HAVE TWO ROLES: **They should visually unite a porch with the architecture of the home and protect the porch from the elements. Although shed roofs are common, easy to build, and complement farmhouse architecture, hip and gable roofs offer greater protection from the weather and complement a wider range of architectural styles.**

Hip roofs overhang on all sides, screening the sun in hot climates and providing the greatest protection from rain. Gable roofs allow more natural light onto porches and feature an attractive triangular roofline, but they provide slightly less protection from sun and rain than hip roofs. For this reason, gable-roofed porches should not face west—the direction from which hard, blowing rains typically prevail.

Shed roof

Gable roof

Hip roof

◄ CAREFUL ATTENTION TO DETAILING results in an outdoor room as attractive as any indoor room. Sealed hardwood floors—rather than the usual painted, stained, or natural flooring planks—enhance this porch, which gives it the polished look of an interior space.

▼ THE 12-IN. BOXED COLUMNS on this porch feature white-stained crown molding, base molding, and decorative railing. The columns not only look great, but also carefully conceal wiring and support electrical outlets that are used for floor lamps.

Lighting a Porch

WHILE CEILING FIXTURES ARE THE MOST COMMON LIGHTING used on a porch, they aren't always the most practical. Because there are no roof cavities in which to hide can-light fixtures, choices are limited to exterior mount and hanging fixtures. Also, overhead lights rarely create the soft ambient light that is so appealing on a porch.

Floor lamps, table lamps, and wall sconces create much softer lighting, but some advanced planning is required for their installation. Prerouting porch posts before construction will allow wiring for light fixtures and electrical outlets to be concealed from view. Header beams can also be prerouted and wired to an electrical switch so that festive string lights can be mounted overhead.

▼ PORCH ADDITIONS LOOK BEST if they are designed to look like part of the home's original architecture rather than as an "enclosed deck." The Prairie-style windows help accomplish that here, as do the boards that enclose the open space beneath the deck.

◀ THIS TRADITIONAL, WOOD-FRAMED CONSERVATORY with glass windows was added to the house to create an elegant sunroom. This sunroom has a glass ceiling, making it an especially bright room for dining, reading, or tending houseplants. Swinging windows allow fresh air inside.

▼ WHEN THESE HOMEOWNERS REALIZED THAT ADDING a screened porch to their house would block light in the living room, they opted for a freestanding porch that includes an upstairs studio. It flows out onto a dry-laid stone patio that connects the house and porch.

▲ THE COMBINATION OF THE BARREL-VAULTED CEILING and flat, dropped ceilings break up this large space, creating sheltered areas for dining and sitting while drawing attention to the mountain view beyond. Broad eaves provide shelter from rainstorms.

◄ TRANSOM WINDOWS, exposed timber rafters, and a vaulted ceiling give this sunroom a sense of height and help form a bright, airy space. The wainscot and uplights draw the eye upward, while the dark tile floors ground the room and give it a sense of warmth.

Balconies and Rooftops

BALCONIES AND ROOFTOPS ARE RARELY SHELTERED, **but like porches and sunrooms, they offer quiet refuges just steps away from a home's** interior living spaces. Balconies are frequently located near bedrooms, so an east or west orientation appropriately affords a view of the sunrise or sunset. They may either extend from the house or be recessed into a nook.

Rooftop patios, while most common above in-town lofts, row houses, or other flat-roofed city buildings, are welcome in any environment where interesting views abound. Although creating a garden on a rooftop usually requires hauling lots of pots, plants, bags of soil, and furnishings up staircases, the results can be well worth the effort—a lush urban oasis from which to enjoy a romantic dinner beneath the stars. Arbors and other garden structures can even be built to create a shady rooftop retreat if desired. Just use sturdy materials and anchor them securely to the roof because they will occasionally be exposed to fierce winds.

▲ BALCONIES ARE USUALLY SMALLER than decks and located off private upstairs quarters, making them excellent places to begin and end the day. The railing on this balcony is just high enough to create a safe environment while permitting views to the bay beyond.

◄ EVEN CITY DWELLERS CAN ENJOY their own outdoor "private" space. The surrounding building walls cast shade and buffer the wind on this rooftop, creating a variable, changing environment, while container plants help green up the space.

▲ SIMPLE, COZY BALCONIES can be added to many rooms without breaking the budget. This one, built just off a master bedroom, is perfect for a couple to unwind before turning in for the night.

Backyard Retreats

EVERYONE NEEDS SPACE IN WHICH TO ESCAPE, if ever so briefly, from the hustle and bustle of daily activities. Depending on your idea of "getting away," a backyard retreat could take the form of a simple garden bench, a Japanese-style teahouse, or an artist's studio. And every landscape, regardless of size, can benefit from a quiet seating area. Whether a teak bench overlooking a pond or a conversation nook in a garden, designating a special spot to unwind will enhance your outdoor experience.

Gazebos and pergolas provide sheltered areas that offer a peaceful sense of enclosure and sanctuary from the outside world. As large structures, they often double as focal points in the landscape. Garages, playhouses, sheds, and custom-built structures can be transformed into studios or workshops and can afford the mental and physical space to really relax. Regardless of what form your ideal retreat takes, comfortable furnishings will ensure that the space is as rejuvenating and versatile as you wish it to be.

▲ RATHER THAN PLACE THIS BENCH randomly along a garden path, it was neatly tucked in among the foliage—making it every bit as important to the garden composition as any of the plants. It provides a quiet place to pause while wandering through the garden.

◄ DUBBED THE "HOLLY HOUSE" by its owners because architectural features and paint colors mimic the leaves and berries of nearby holly bushes, this freestanding structure is a screened porch in the woods where the family can get out of the house without going too far.

▲ LANDSCAPING SLOPED SITES can be challenging, as structures require solid foundations, and access trails call for carefully placed steps. Here, a large pavilion was built on a steep hillside overlooking a waterfall. It was carefully tucked into the woods to avoid disturbing too many trees.

GAZEBOS AND PERGOLAS

▲ THE OCTAGONAL FAÇADE, turreted roof, and arched openings make this screened gazebo a focal point in the backyard. The siding, trim, and roofing materials match those of the house, lending a sense of unity to the landscape.

◄ PERGOLAS WERE ORIGINALLY DESIGNED as covered passageways but quickly evolved into destinations of their own. This pergola spans a raised walkway, yet it is wide enough for a couple of wicker rockers, which offer an excellent viewing point in the garden.

▲ WINDOWPANES ADD TO THE ROOMLIKE ATMOSPHERE
of this pergola. The entire structure is tucked neatly into a
mixed shrub and perennial border, making it a favorite garden
getaway, as well as a place for the gardener to take a short break.

▲ NESTLED IN A WOODLAND GARDEN, the temperature in this gazebo is considerably cooler than in the sun on a hot summer day. The roof provides shelter from sun and rain, while a latticed section helps keep shrubs from reaching into the sitting area.

▶ ALTHOUGH NOT VERY COMMON TODAY, gazebos—structures originally designed for gazing—are often built in the form of turrets, echoing architectural elements of an accompanying home. The sides of this gazebo are designed to look like large windows for gazing.

▶ **THIS ASIAN-STYLE PAVILION** is not overly large, yet it easily accommodates six chairs around a central table. Side-panel drapes can be closed for added privacy or to provide screening from light breezes or unexpected rain showers.

▼ **THIS WELL-PROPORTIONED** and thoughtfully detailed gazebo is small enough to tuck into an urban backyard but large enough to seat four for dinner or a game of cards. The decorative railing, corner brackets, shingled roof, and cupola make it an eye-catching addition to the landscape.

Upgrading Gazebo Floors

GAZEBO FLOORS ARE MOST COMMONLY constructed from decking wood, but flagstone, tile, brick, or concrete pavers laid on a slab can also be used. They require minimal maintenance and will remain beautiful for years. Decorative concrete that has been stained or textured can provide character.

▶ STRIKING REFLECTIONS CAN BE CREATED by placing architectural structures near water features with dark interiors. The combo here works in concert to provide stunning views and a soothing setting that is conducive to quiet activities. The old tree contributes to this scene.

▼ TODAY'S GARDEN STRUCTURES are often hybrids of pergolas, arbors, pavilions, and gazebos—incorporating the best elements of each. This open-roofed structure, which spans a deck, clearly defines a casual area for dining and enjoying the views, while providing support for flowering vines.

▲ ANYTHING WHITE IN THE LANDSCAPE is the first thing to catch the eye—so this gazebo is, appropriately, the focal point of the backyard garden. Two intricately pruned topiaries mark the entrance to the gazebo, keeping with the formal design of the structure.

Keeping Cool

ALTHOUGH PERGOLAS, GAZEBOS, AND PAVILIONS ARE OFTEN ADDED for their structural and aesthetic contributions to a landscape, their original purpose, dating back to Roman times, was to provide a cool place to relax on a hot day. While the structures themselves offer some shade, their cooling abilities can be enhanced by adding a solid roof (which also sheds rain), creating a leafy canopy overhead with dense vines, or adding ceiling fans.

Shading south- and west-facing walls with lattice or dense plantings can also help lower temperatures by as much as 10°F on a hot summer day. By building pergolas adjacent to a house, indoor temperatures can be lowered, too.

GARDEN SEATING

▲ BENCHES MADE OF NATURAL MATERIALS blend almost seamlessly into the landscape. This one was made from large stone slabs, but a single large boulder or even a tree stump would provide an equally enchanting place to pause while exploring the garden.

▲ BENCHES CAN BE PLACED along the edge of a lawn like this one, along a path, or overlooking a special view. Because this bench accommodates a basket of flowers, it encourages sitting alone rather than with family or friends.

▶ A SITTING AREA WAS CREATED in this garden by simply widening the path by a few feet. The rustic twig furniture maintains the naturalistic feel, but it can be uncomfortable; weatherproof fabric cushions solve this problem, while adding pattern and color that complement the plantings.

▲ A CONVERSATION NOOK with garden benches and chairs was created in this small boxwood parterre, or patterned garden. Although it is located adjacent to the house, it is out of the main flow of traffic, ensuring a quiet place to relax.

Creating the Perfect Area

DIFFERENT PEOPLE LIKE SITTING IN DIFFERENT ENVIRONMENTS. Some enjoy the warmth of the sun; others prefer a shady canopy. Some embrace open spaces with expansive views; others settle more comfortably into cozy nooks. Some like feeling as if they are sitting on top of the world; others seek the security of a sunken garden.

Before settling on the location for a seating area, try this trick: Each day, place a folding chair in a different location, sit there awhile, and take note of how it feels. Keep moving the chair around until you find just the right spot for a more permanent bench or cluster of chairs.

▶ LIKE MOST COZY SEATING AREAS, this one has a backdrop and sense of enclosure. The rough stone retaining wall also provides a striking counterpoint to the smooth surface of the teak benches. As the Latin inscription on the chairs proclaims: "Behold how good." Indeed!

▼ NATURALLY ROT-RESISTANT WOODS such as teak, cedar, and redwood are good choices for benches that will remain outside year-round. The design of this teak bench is particularly suitable for the contemporary house style and casual landscape.

Warm Hearths

NOTHING KNOCKS THE CHILL OFF A COOL EVENING faster than a blazing fire. In fact, outdoor hearths can be even more inviting than indoor hearths because temperature swings are greater outdoors. Outdoor hearths create the kind of ambience that transforms a typical evening into a memorable one, and they can extend the season for outdoor living.

Outdoor hearths come in all shapes and sizes—from fire pits, fire dishes, chimineas, and luminaries to full-sized and oversized fireplaces with mantels, raised hearths, and chimneys. They may be custom built on site, installed as modular prefabricated components, or delivered as ready-to-light units. For porches and sunrooms with interior walls, vent-free fireplaces are an appealing option. Finishing materials run the gamut from stone, brick, and stucco to colorful, decorative tile. Fuel sources include wood and gas, as well as alternative fuels such as wax-based logs, pellets, and gels.

▶ THIS RUSTIC STONE FIREPLACE shares a chimney with an indoor fireplace—a smart money-saving strategy. A ledge was built into the brick firebox, allowing a grilling rack to be placed over the fire for cooking.

▼ IN WARM CLIMATES, a fireplace is more for ambience than warmth, but it can knock off the chill on a damp day. These vented gas logs are a good choice, as they look like burning logs but put out less heat than ventless logs or firewood.

◀ THIS CUSTOM-BUILT STUCCO FIREPLACE doubles as a patio wall, defining one boundary of an outdoor room. Built-in storage bins keep firewood dry and convenient. This area, with the formal fireplace, traditional seating arrangement, and patterned floor, demonstrates how you can capture an indoor feeling outdoors.

▲ FIREWOOD IS CONVENIENTLY STACKED to the right of this fireplace. Allowed to dry for six months, the wood will light easily and burn hot. If well-seasoned wood isn't available, wax-based fire logs, which reduce emissions by up to two-thirds, are a smart environmental alternative.

◄ RECTANGULAR SPACES OFFER GREATER FLEXIBILITY for arranging furniture. The size and shape of this space allows for two seating areas—a warm conversation area near the fireplace, plus a nearby dining area that still benefits from the ambience created by the fireplace.

▼ A GAS-FUELED FIRE PIT warms this patio seating area, which offers all the comforts of informality while still being chic. A wooden bench and Adirondack chairs have been pulled up around the fire pit as if it were a campfire, forming a casual conversation area.

Evolution of the Modern Fireplace

TRADITIONAL MASONRY FIREPLACES are going the way of the dinosaur as more affordable, energy-efficient models made from premanufactured modular masonry sections take their place. Another new option, a wood-framed fireplace with metal firebox and chimney, is even more affordable but less energy efficient than a modular masonry fireplace.

Both styles are widely available, easily installed, and offer a choice of wood-burning, direct-vent gas, and vent-free gas units. Vent-free models, built with technology similar to that of gas stoves, are good choices where it would be difficult to build a chimney. The fireplace surrounds on all models may be dressed up with brick, stone, tile, or stucco.

◄ THIS OUTDOOR ROOM is located in a courtyard pavilion that has solid walls along two sides. This wall features a fireplace with a stone façade and hearth that imitate the look of an indoor room. An outdoor kitchen is built into the adjoining wall.

▲ THIS PORTABLE FIRE PIT burns either charcoal or small logs. It is ideal for tight spaces and can be easily moved to a new location. The rounded cover acts as a fire screen, and a grill rack can be laid on top for cooking.

► A FREESTANDING STUCCO FIREPLACE is built into a curved seating wall, making it the focal point of the backyard patio and an inviting place to gather around. Candles can be placed on the recessed and stone-ledge shelves for added ambience and soft lighting.

▲ IN-GROUND AND CONTAINER GARDENS with roses, herbs, and citrus trees partially enclose this generous brick patio to create a relaxed atmosphere around the fireplace. A separate area for dining is located nearby, adjacent to both indoor and outdoor kitchens.

▲ THE STURDY, WISTERIA-DRAPED ARBOR helps identify the upper and outer boundaries of this outdoor room, which is anchored by a large, traditional masonry fireplace. The brick chimney extends slightly above the arbor, venting smoke away and preventing any harm to the vine.

▶ THE STONE USED IN THE FLOOR, walls, fireplace, and pool are the unifying element in this patio. The walls and fireplace, along with the painted arbor, define the seating area, while the pool contributes to a relaxing atmosphere. The walls provide ample seating when entertaining.

Heat Where You Need It

A PRACTICAL AND AFFORDABLE ALTERNATIVE **to fireplaces and fire pits is the patio** heater. Fueled by either natural gas or propane, patio heaters come in tabletop and floor models and with stainless steel or painted finishes. Most have adjustable heat output and easy-to-use ignition starters. Look for a sturdy model with safety valves that shut off the unit automatically if it is tilted.

Patio heaters are designed primarily for use in open spaces. If used beneath a structure, be sure there is a high, flame-retardant roof overhead and excellent ventilation. Patio heaters may be connected to natural gas lines or fueled with propane tanks for greater portability.

▶ IF YOU DON'T HAVE THE SPACE, budget, or inclination for an outdoor hearth but want the heating benefits, consider a portable heater. This one burns natural gas. It has a heavy base to prevent it from tipping over and a flared cap that radiates heat in a 20-ft. radius. Smaller tabletop models, as well as propane models, are also available.

▲ A BROAD BRICK FIREPLACE doubles as a retaining wall along the hillside. The wall also offers built-in cabinets and bluestone counters that can be used for gardening or entertaining needs. The brick chimney is just high enough to direct smoke away from the patio.

▶ THIS GROUND-LEVEL FIRE PIT features two ring burners—round, steel pipes that can be connected to natural gas or propane and that are slightly buried beneath a nonflammable surface, such as gravel or lava rocks—to create a unique, multiflame effect.

▲ THE PAINTED WALLS, hardwood floors, and gas fireplace form a warm, comfortable setting on this porch that makes it feel like a family room. The wooden mantel and tile surround on the hearth add to the roomlike atmosphere, while ceiling fans keep warm air circulating.

◄ MODERN FIRE PITS, while diverse in style and character, are inspired by rustic council rings or campfire circles that were popular in the early 1900s as gathering places for song, dance, and storytelling. This one overlooks the surrounding countryside and features built-in seating.

▲ THE STACKED-STONE FIRE PIT matches the surrounding stone patio. Its circular shape is emphasized by the elegant, curved bench. The simple design and materials, as well as the mostly green, massed plantings, create a soothing atmosphere for relaxing around the fire.

◄ A SIMPLY CON-STRUCTED FIRE PIT is surrounded by a round patio and a rhododendron- and azalea-filled garden. It was constructed by leaving a graveled clearing in the center of the patio, which is encircled by rocks to contain a small, wood-burning fire.

▲ THIS BROAD STONE HEARTH offers casual seating beneath a large pavilion, which is well suited for relaxed gatherings with friends or family. The chimney for the wood-burning fireplace extends outside and above the pavilion to keep the space from filling with smoke.

◄ THE DECK FLOOR DOUBLES AS SEATING for this sunken campfire area, located just a few feet from the outdoor bedroom (the structure in the background). Wood-burning fire pits are a good do-it-yourself weekend project for homeowners with basic masonry skills.

► THIS GAS-BURNING FIRE PIT anchors one corner of a small backyard patio. The stone in the raised fire pit matches that of the surrounding seat wall, as well as the stepping stones through the lawn. A high wall offers privacy in a neighborhood setting.

▼ KILN-FIRED, WOOD-BURNING CLAY CHIMINEAS are both affordable and ideal for small spaces. Because chimineas are portable, homeowners can take them along if they move, or they can be repositioned on decks, patios, or other open-air spaces for different occasions.

A Clean Burn

TRADITIONAL OPEN-COMBUSTION WOOD-BURNING FIREPLACES with their flickering flames and crackling sounds certainly offer the greatest ambience, but they aren't very energy efficient. Clean-burning and Environmental Protection Agency-certified (EPA) wood-burning fireplaces—insulated, closed-combustion units with glass doors—put out more heat and generate less air pollution.

If watching flames through glass isn't your idea of ambience, burning well-seasoned firewood (dried for at least six months) or manufactured logs will help reduce wood smoke emissions. Traditional open-combustion fireplaces can be made more efficient by adding cast-iron or steel inserts that burn wood, natural gas, propane, pellets, or coal. Be sure to comply with any local regulations regarding fireplaces and fuels.

▼ SHARING A CHIMNEY with an indoor one, this fireplace features a uniquely shaped firebox opening. The surrounding white walls and dramatic arched entry form a bright and inviting courtyard setting that has been transformed into a striking outdoor room.

Outdoor Recreation

Outdoor recreation has advanced significantly in the last couple of decades, evolving from tire swings and sprinklers to elaborate play structures, game courts, and virtual water parks. And it's not just the kids who have benefited; adults are getting in on the action and discovering a more invigorating version of family time. Whether it's your dream to gather around a pool or turn your backyard into a back nine, options abound for every whim.

Since backyard recreation is now for kids of all ages, it's important to include something for each member of the family. Begin by providing safe play spaces for young children that can be easily viewed from indoors. Older children still need to be within earshot, but they appreciate a bit more privacy, perhaps a tree house or game court located farther from the house. Teens often enjoy group activities—anything from roller hockey and skateboarding to soccer and basketball—or they may need a place to practice their jump shots and pitching for the school team.

Adults tend to combine recreation and entertaining, so place putting greens, croquet courts, or an outdoor pool table near the patio. And, of course, friends and family will enjoy spending time around a pool—whether it's swimming laps, playing water volleyball, or just soaking up the sun.

◄ A VARIETY OF GATHERING PLACES makes this swimming pool a favorite destination any time of day. The broad pool deck is ideal for sunning or entertaining, the arbor casts shade over a dining area, and the pool house provides shelter from wind or sudden rain showers.

Architectural Pools

AN ARCHITECTURAL POOL IS A CUSTOM-BUILT SWIMMING POOL that has been designed in such a way that it has an undeniable relationship with the accompanying house. At times, it may even be difficult to distinguish where the house ends and the pool begins. More often, however, the house and pool are separate and distinct elements that relate to one another through their alignment and use of construction materials. On occasion, the pool itself is a striking architectural element in the landscape, with strong lines and bold geometric shapes. For these reasons, it's not surprising that architectural pools are frequently designed by architects and constructed at the same time as the house.

Architectural pools are typically placed close to the house, with a pool deck or terrace doubling as a transitional space between the two. Paving materials may flow from indoor rooms out onto the pool deck, and large expanses of windows may overlook the pool area.

▼ MODULAR SHAPES, CLEAN LINES, AND SIMPLE materials are used in the design and construction of both this house and pool. They are further united by a transitional deck, which extends from the walls of the house all the way to the pool's edge.

◄ BY PAYING CLOSE ATTENTION TO details, even a small pool can make a strong architectural statement in the landscape. This one is raised to a comfortable seating height and accented by a raised deck. The bold color contrast between the pool's interior and its surrounds is also eye-catching.

► THE REPETITION OF CIRCULAR elements lends this landscape a sense of formality and intrigue. Circles can be found in the pool itself, the spa, the steps leading into the pool, and the brick retaining walls that surround the pool and spa.

Budgeting Basics

Building a pool is like remodeling or adding a new room onto your house. Industry experts suggest budgeting around 15 percent of your total property value on the pool and surrounding landscape, or as much as 20 percent if you include a poolhouse or other special features. If your property is valued at $300,000, you can expect to spend around $45,000 on an in-ground pool and landscaping.

▲ IN CONTRAST TO THE UNUSUAL, sloping angles of the roofline, the rest of the house speaks to a sense of simplicity in its overall design, materials, and landscaping. The simplicity of the pool, deck, and plantings echoes the design of the house. Yet, like the roofline, the pool sits at an angle to the house to give the composition of the backyard an element of surprise.

▲ THIS POOL WAS BUILT WHERE A COURTYARD WOULD TRADITIONALLY BE located. As a result, it can be viewed from several surrounding rooms through floor-to-ceiling windows and sliding-glass doors. A breezeway connects these rooms by passing over the water like a bridge.

◄ THE OWNER OF THIS POOL STARTED with a simple rectangular design and then altered it on each side with nooks and crannies to create a distinctive design. The tiered, aboveground decking makes the pool site architecturally interesting and offers additional places to entertain.

▲ AN IRREGULARLY SHAPED POOL RADIATES out from this house. The wide steps descend from the back terrace and continue into the pool, creating continuity between the deck, steps, and pool.

▶ THE STONE-AND-CONCRETE FOUNDATION of this house doubles as an interior wall for the pool. Bringing the water this close to the house creates a stunning view through the floor-to-ceiling windows, while water casts reflections on the interior walls of the house, creating a sense of light and movement throughout the day.

Who Designs Pools?

ARCHITECTS, landscape architects, landscape designers, and pool builders all design pools. Consult an architect if you are building both a house and a pool, adding a poolhouse, or if your site poses unusual engineering challenges. A landscape architect or landscape designer can help design a pool that blends with an existing home, as well as design the surrounding landscape. Many pool builders have architects or landscape architects on staff that can design custom pools; others offer off-the-shelf plans that may better suit a limited budget.

▼ DOUBLE DECKS CREATE GATHERING PLACES BESIDE this pool. The upper deck serves as a transitional space, while the lower deck provides a platform from which to enter and exit the pool. The rectangular pattern in the deck tiles and windows ties it all together.

FOUNTAINS AND CASCADES

▼ BY PLACING A WATER FEATURE NEAR the house, its gentle, soothing sounds can be enjoyed both indoors and around the pool. A sheet waterfall has been placed beneath this bedroom window, where it helps the homeowners ease into a good night's sleep.

▶ FIBER OPTIC LIGHTS ILLUMINATE THESE arching jets of water, while a computer-controlled color wheel automatically changes their color, creating a theatrical poolside performance. Laminar-flow jets, which create the arches, are positioned away from the pool so that the water shoots up and over the pool deck and into the water.

► THOUGH THE HIGH MASONRY WALL buffers some sound, it is more effective as a privacy wall and windscreen. Splashing water does a much better job of masking the surrounding neighborhood noise. A generous flow of water pours through flumes, churning into the lap pool below.

◄ WATER APPEARS TO CASCADE OVER THE DAM OF A SMALL canal, but closer inspection reveals that water is actually forced through a series of small holes, creating a sheet waterfall that flows into a naturalistic pool.

The Sound of Water

RUNNING WATER is one of the most relaxing sounds in any landscape—which is why water features in pools are so popular. Of course, all types of running water do not sound the same. You can achieve the desired sound effect by adjusting the volume of water, the distance that it falls, and the surface over which it falls. A rule of thumb: The greater the volume of water and the greater the distance it falls, the louder the sound it makes.

The Water-Wise Pool

WATER HAS BECOME a scarce resource in many fast-growing communities and regions with limited rainfall. As a result, some municipalities have placed restrictions on water use for pools. To cooperate with water-conservation practices, build your pool only as large and as deep as needed for anticipated activities and don't automatically empty your pool at the end of the season. In most cases, water can be left in pools over the winter, even in cold climates.

◀ SPRAY-JET NOZZLES CAN CREATE a variety of fountain effects. Streaming jets, like this one, can produce single or multiple streams of water at varied heights. Fanning jets produce a clear sheet of water that is best suited to sheltered, windless sites.

▶ WATER MOVES MORE SLOWLY AND MAKES less noise when entering this pool after traveling down a rough, sloping, split-rock surface than it would cascading through a flume or over a straight ledge. However, the slow trickle of water can be as hypnotic in sight and sound as a crashing cascade.

▲ THE STEPS LEADING INTO THIS POOL double as a waterfall. There's no need to worry about slippery stone steps because the pool's chlorinated water prevents the buildup of algae.

◄ WATER SPILLS CONTINUOUSLY FROM the spa into the pool below through a narrow cutout. It has a distinctive sound, like that of water being poured from a bucket into a pool of water.

Naturalistic Pools

IN CONTRAST TO THE STRONG LINES OF AN ARCHITECTURAL POOL, a naturalistic swimming pool is designed to blend almost seamlessly into its
surrounding landscape. It is commonly placed at a greater distance
from the house, often along a woodland edge or at a low point where
you might expect to find a pond. In fact, most naturalistic pools mimic
ponds or lagoons in their free-form shape, and they are often enhanced
with trickling streams and cascading waterfalls. The pool's edges may
be anchored with boulders and planting pockets, or they may descend
gradually down into the water from dry land, resembling a sandy beach.

◄ WITH NO SIGN OF ANY MANMADE EDGES, THIS SMALL
pool looks like a natural spring. The stepping-stones
and lush carpet of soft, creeping ground covers
enhance the woodland setting.

▼ THE ABUNDANT BOULDERS CREATE A NATURALISTIC
environment around this free-form pool. The
random stone paving, recirculating stream, and
garden paths help create a natural-looking setting.

◄ DESIGNED IN THE 1970S BY RENOWNED landscape architect Thomas Church, this pool was among the first naturalistic swimming pools. The dark bottom allows the boulders and grasses tucked around the pool's edges to be reflected in the water.

▲ ALTHOUGH THIS OVAL POOL HAS A MORTARED, CUT-STONE EDGE, ITS small size, its position at the bottom of a hill under the shade of trees, and the surrounding landscape all work together to create the appearance of a small pond.

Before You Dig

BUILDING A SWIMMING POOL requires construction—an activity that almost always interests local officials, utility companies, and neighbors. Before you break ground, check your zoning laws, building codes, health and safety codes, property deed, and subdivision covenants for any restrictions, easements, setbacks, or safety requirements. Identify the location of any septic tanks, rock ledges, and underground utilities that could affect where you place your pool, and make absolutely sure that this information is relayed to your pool designer and builder.

▼ THE WOODLAND, WHICH IS VIEWED THROUGH THE ARBOR, creates a natural backdrop for this pool. The concrete decking faces the lawn and the house and creates a subtle transition from the manmade poolscape to the natural landscape beyond.

▼ DENSE PLANTINGS OBSCURE A WOODEN FENCE, transforming this space into a naturalistic setting. Paths wind naturally around planting pockets near the pool's edge.

◀ THIS POOL LOOKS LIKE A LAGOON. The effect is achieved with a freeform shape, a natural-looking edge, a textured bottom resembling sand, turquoise water reflecting off the pool's interior, and tropical plantings. A hammock strung between palm trees adds an appropriate finishing touch to the setting.

▲ THE POOL, POSITIONED AT THE rear of the property, along the woodland edge, beckons guests as they catch a glance of it from inside the house. Because it is placed at a distance from the house, the pool becomes the prime—and much anticipated— destination of the backyard.

Recycling Excavated Soil

WHEN INSTALLING an in-ground pool, your contractors will have to remove many truckloads of soil. Rather than pay to have the soil hauled off, consider using it elsewhere in your landscape to create rolling terrain or mounds, which are especially appropriate around a naturalistic pool or spa. You can use mounds in the design of waterfalls and gently falling streams as well as to plant raised wind buffers and screening.

FALLING WATER

▲ THE STEEP SLOPE OF THIS SITE PROVIDED THE homeowners with an opportunity to design a series of small pools with a waterfall. The waterfall spills into a small pond adjacent to, but separate from, the swim area and spa. Each pool has tile edging for seating.

▲ ONE OF THE KEYS TO MAKING A RECIRCULATING WATERFALL LOOK NATURAL IS camouflaging the water's origin. Dense, fast-growing ornamental grasses do the trick here.

◄ A WELL-POSITIONED SPOTLIGHT ILLUMINATES THIS SPA'S WATERFALL AT NIGHT. The water cascades down four steps, making the homeowners feel as though they are enjoying a dip in a secluded mountain hot spring.

► THE ROUGH-CUT EDGES OF STACKED STONES HAVE AN APPEALING, AGED LOOK, even when newly installed. The cascading water and therapeutic spa make this setting even more inviting.

► A GRADE CHANGE, WHETHER A NATURAL HILLSIDE OR A MANMADE MOUND, is essential for creating a waterfall, while boulders help hold the soil in place. The bottom third of these boulders was buried so that they appear natural in the landscape.

Artificial Stone

Removing stones and boulders from the landscape to place around the pool is not only a labor-intensive and expensive job, but it also often leaves behind environmental problems, such as erosion or the altered flow of rivers where rocks are removed. Artificial stone is an environmentally friendly and less expensive alternative to the real thing, and because artificial stones are lightweight, they are much easier to move into place around a pool. A good craftsman can make faux-stone boulders look and feel real to the touch.

Lap Pools

SWIMMING IS AN EXCELLENT LOW-IMPACT AEROBIC EXERCISE, as mentally relaxing as it is physically invigorating. For those who desire a pool for fitness purposes, lap pools are an excellent option. Efficient in size and suitable to most lots, lap pools holds less water than most recreational pools and, because of their simple design—little more than a long, narrow lane for swimming—complement almost any architectural style. Any lap pool that is 40 to 75 ft. long, 8 to 10 ft. wide, and at least 3½ ft. deep should satisfy most swimmers. For those who want to do more than swim laps, an unobstructed swimming lane can be designated in a larger recreational pool.

◄ A COVERED POOL ALLOWS FOR swimming, rain or shine. The open sides of the structure allow fresh air to circulate. This single-lane lap pool features steps built into the side and a ladder for easy exits. Nearby closets conceal the pool equipment.

▲ THIS L-SHAPED LAP POOL OFFERS THE
best of both worlds: a long lane
for swimming plus a wider area for
recreation that is suitable for water
sports and relaxing on floats.

Steps for Lap Pools

OR SAFETY AND CONVENIENCE, the steps in a lap pool
should be designed so that they do not inter-
fere with swimming. The walls at the ends of
the lane should remain flat and parallel to accommodate flip turns. In a narrow, single-lane lap pool, the
ladder should be recessed into the sidewall, with a
handrail built into the deck for support. In a wider lap
pool, narrow steps can be placed along one side—just
mark both the swimming lane and steps with paint
or tile to help swimmers stay on course. You can also
extend a section of the pool to accommodate steps.
In fact, these extensions add a decorative element to
an otherwise simple pool design. When a lap pool is
part of a larger, multipurpose pool, build steps and
ladders away from the lanes.

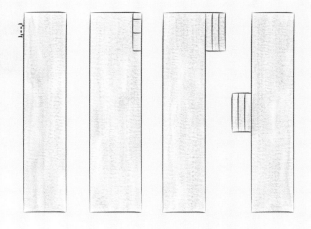

◀ THE OWNERS OF THIS SHALLOW LOT made excellent use of their space by tucking in a long, narrow lap pool. Steps are placed near both ends for convenience.

▼ ONE OF THE CHARMS OF LAP POOLS is their simple design. Most are long and linear, such as this pool, which makes a strong visual statement in the landscape. It accentuates the linearity of this outdoor room.

▼ THE DESIGNER OF THIS LAP POOL CREATED AN EXTENSION on one side so the steps would be out of the swim lanes. Such extensions can also be placed at the center of one side of a lap pool or designed as semi-circular spaces rather than rectangles.

Swim Spas

A SWIM SPA CAN PROVIDE A COMPACT ALTERNATIVE to a lap pool. Swim spas—sometimes called jet pools—are small pools with adjustable water jets that create a current and allow you to swim in place—much like jogging on a treadmill. By adjusting these jets, you can increase the intensity of your workout and accommodate swimmers with different skill, endurance, and strength levels.

Many swim spas double as spas with massaging hydrojets. Allow enough time for the water to heat up or cool down between activities. The ideal water temperature is 78°F to 82°F for swimming and 98°F to 104°F for hydrotherapy. An alternative is to build a swim spa with two areas—one for swimming and one for relaxing—each with its own temperature control.

Swim spas occupy much less space and use less water than lap pools, yet are larger than most spas. They average 13 to 20 ft. long and can be easily tucked into even the tiniest of backyards. Most are 3½ to 4 ft. deep, but deeper models are available for water aerobics.

▲ LIKE OTHER TYPES OF POOL, SWIM SPAS ARE AVAILABLE IN ASSORTED SHAPES AND SIZES. Spas are smaller and easier to tuck into a hillside than a full-size pool. This kidney-shaped swim spa fits naturally into a sloped yard that overlooks a nearby lake.

Recreational Pools

THE MOST POPULAR POOLS ARE THOSE DESIGNED FOR A VARIETY of recreational activities—from floating and swimming to water volleyball and diving. Recreational pools can be built in any shape, size, or style and often include coves for wading or for children's play. Although most recreational pools are 3½ ft. to 5 ft. deep, the depth of a pool can vary from one end to the other. For diving, one end of the pool should be at least 11 ft. deep. For games and water aerobics, a 4-ft.-deep area is ideal for keeping everyone's heads above water. Special features, such as waterfalls, slides, and underwater benches, make hanging out by the pool a favorite family pastime.

▼ THIS KIDNEY-SHAPED RECREATIONAL pool is small enough to tuck into a side yard on a sloped lot with room to spare for brick decking and poolside planting pockets.

◄ CAREFUL MAINTENANCE CAN EXTEND THE LIFE OF A VINYL liner. This one lasted for 20 years before it had to be replaced. The broad end of this lazy-L-shaped pool is 11 ft. deep, which is considered a safe depth for diving.

► A BROAD DECK ON ONE SIDE OF THIS RECTANGULAR pool offers plenty of space for lounge chairs and tables. With the surrounding lush gardens enhancing the setting, this pool area also serves as a cool, restful spot for entertaining.

Building an In-Ground Pool

IN-GROUND POOLS COME IN THREE BASIC construction types: concrete, vinyl-lined, and fiberglass. A concrete pool—whether poured, gunite, shot-crete, or masonry block—is highly durable, can be built in almost any shape or size imaginable, and can be finished in a wide variety of colors, textures, or tiled patterns. A vinyl-lined or fiber-glass pool—although limited in shape, size, and finish—costs less, can be installed quickly, and provides a good alternative for cold climates where a concrete pool could crack without special reinforcement.

▼ THIS POOL COULD BE DESIGNED IN ANY SHAPE IMAGINED BY THE homeowners because a custom frame was built on site and then filled with concrete. In contrast, vinyl-lined or fiberglass pools are typically offered in a limited range of shapes and sizes.

▼ A DIVING BOARD OFFERS HOURS of enjoyment for swimmers. For safety, diving boards should extend out over deep water and be located away from slides, steps, and other recreational equipment.

◄ THIS MULTIFUNCTIONAL POOL features several activity areas, along with an underwater bench on the right side. Plantings provide shady relief for swimmers who prefer to stay in the water but need a short rest from the rays.

▼ LOCATED AWAY FROM THE HOUSE and down a flight of stone steps, as part of a garden, this pool is designed as a destination area. A multitude of gathering spaces are offered, both in and out of water. Shallow steps that run the width of one end of the pool and an underwater bench on the right side of the pool offer ample in-the-water seating.

Dive Safely

Despite growing safety concerns, diving is still a popular swimming pool activity. The keys to diving safely include having plenty of deep-water pool area and proper supervision. Though standards vary, safety organizations recommend at least 11 ft. of water beneath the board, with the deep end extending at least 16 ft. from the board into the middle of the pool. Short jump boards, which offer limited spring, and fixed-platform diving rocks are gaining in popularity over traditional, longer diving boards.

Updating Existing Pools

ANY POOL CAN BE UPGRADED, though major changes—such as converting from a vinyl-lined pool to a concrete one—can cost as much as installing a new pool. To refresh your pool, consider expanding or resurfacing the deck, changing the coping around the pool's edge, updating the interior finish, or adding special features such as spas, waterfalls, fountains, and swim-up bars. Other options for enhancing your poolside setting include arbors, pool-houses, or outdoor kitchens.

▲ SUNBATHING IS A PRIORITY AROUND this pool. In addition to the chaise lounges, the convex spaces at each end of the pool increase the room for floats. The lush green grass gives swimmers' feet cooling relief.

◄ THIS POOL GENTLY WRAPS AROUND the corner of the house, leaving plenty of room for an exuberant garden. The proximity of the pool to the house increases the homeowners' use of the space, whether for swimming or outdoor entertaining.

▲ THIS BACKYARD IS A GATHERING
space with the swimming pool
as the focal point. The boulders
and naturalistic plantings set
the mood for hours of entertaining in nature.

Shaped to Suit Your Style

IF YOU CAN IMAGINE A POOL SHAPE, someone can build it. So how do you settle on a shape? The layout of your house or shape of your lot is often the driving factor behind choosing a pool design. Your setting is important, too. Pools with geometric shapes tend to suit traditional homes and landscapes, while free-form pools are called for in more casual settings. Rectangular pools, still a popular option, support a wide range of activities and are easily equipped with automatic covers. But in the end, it's often a simple matter of personal preference.

COMMON POOL SHAPES

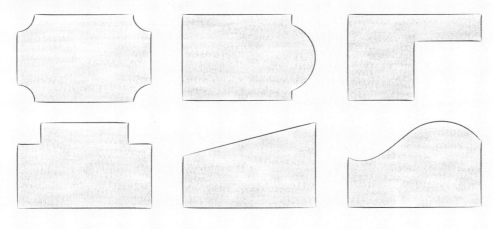

SMALL POOLS

◄ THE SMALLER THE LOT, THE SIMPLER the shape of the pool should be. The homeowner of this tiny yard and pool created an inviting, intimate setting by cultivating tall garden walls and planting lush greenery.

▼ IMAGINE TAKING AN AFTERNOON walk and stumbling upon this perfectly round pool set against a natural hillside. Because the home-owners designed the area to be a quiet retreat rather than a recre-ational spot, they eliminated the need for a traditional pool deck.

Take the Plunge

PLUNGE POOLS—small, shallow pools intended for lounging rather than for swimming—are growing in popularity due to their lower cost, smaller size, and reduced water needs. Especially suited to a small site, plunge pools can also be tucked into small corners on larger lots. Because plunge pools are small, it is often possible to upgrade the materials or add a water feature without exceeding your budget.

▲ THIS SMALL POOL DOES DOUBLE duty as a garden feature. The oval design, which helps the pool blend into the surrounding formal landscape, provides a place to cool off during a hot summer afternoon.

▶ THIS PINT-SIZE POOL PACKS A LOT of impact. It contains an elevated spa, multiple waterfalls, and an underwater bench. A small, raised lawn for sunbathing overlooks the pool. The brick steps and walls connect the pool to the house, which is built from the same material.

ABOVEGROUND POOLS

▼ IN FENCED BACKYARDS, SHALLOW ABOVEGROUND POOLS can be subtly screened with the strategic placement of loose shrubbery, clipped hedges, and other plantings. The low-growing shrubs surrounding this pool camouflage the pool's base while still offering clear views of the pool for safety.

▲ THE WHITE FENCING AND WHITE OUTDOOR FURNITURE GIVE A sense of unity to this white-edged pool. The interior steps and safety railing are also white. Decking surrounds the pool, making it feel more like an in-ground pool and offering plenty of space for gathering and sunbathing.

Aboveground Advantages

◄ THOUGH MOST ABOVEGROUND POOLS ARE MADE OF METAL, this one features a wooden exterior that is as attractive as it is functional. It also features a small deck for seating and pool access.

▼ A SLOPED SITE CAN ACCOMODATE AN ABOVE-GROUND pool when the land is minimally graded to create a level base. If the pool is positioned so that the upside rim is only slightly above ground level, decking can create the illusion of an in-ground pool.

AN ABOVEGROUND POOL offers several advantages over an in-ground pool. The most significant consideration is its substantially lower price tag. For this reason, many homeowners try out an aboveground pool before investing in a permanent, in-ground pool. An aboveground pool can be constructed in a matter of days, instead of the weeks required to build an in-ground pool. It is also a good choice for rocky landscapes where excavation can be difficult. Because many are portable, some homeowners take their aboveground pools with them when they move.

Spas

SPAS HAVE COME A LONG WAY FROM THE WOODEN-BARREL HOT TUBS OF THE 1960s, but soaking in hot water still offers the same benefits: relaxation, improved circulation, and relief for tired, aching muscles. In addition to hot tubs, choices include portable and prefabricated spas, as well as in-ground, concrete spas. Today's spas feature flexible seating arrangements, high-pressure massaging jets, and computerized temperature controls. A few even come with their own sound systems. A spa can be designed as a stand-alone unit or integrated with a pool to take advantage of shared water and filtration systems. To reap the greatest benefits of a spa, keep the water temperature between 99°F and 104°F.

▼ THIS GENTLY SLOPING SITE ENABLED THE spa to be placed so that it overlooks the pool. When working on a sloped site, it's important to consider how raised decks or retaining walls might be used as jumping platforms by swimmers, and to either place them further from the pool or increase the pool depth accordingly.

◄ CONCRETE SPAS, SUCH AS THIS crescent-shaped one, offer the greatest design flexibility because custom forms allow the concrete to be shaped in any number of ways. Prefabricated spas, while limited in shape and size, tend to feature more comfortable seating.

▲ SPAS CAN BE PLACED EITHER ABOVE OR IN THE GROUND. THIS aboveground spa has a wide rim that doubles as a seating area and can be used as a resting place for towels and amenities.

▲ A SPA PLACED ADJACENT TO A POOL DOESN'T TAKE UP INTERIOR POOL space but can still share a water-circulation system.

▲ THE HOMEOWNERS PLACED THIS SPA A SHORT DASH FROM indoors so they could kick back in the warm water on chilly evenings. Potted plants sit safely along the spa's rim.

► THIS SQUARE SPA IS LOCATED NEAR the house where it benefits from increased privacy. The home's walls also buffer chilling winds during evening soaks. The dark stone rim absorbs heat from the sun for a warm, comfortable seating area.

▶ A NOOK WAS CREATED FOR THIS SPA in a corner next to the pool and cabana where it offers greater privacy and feels more intimate nestled between two columns.

▼ ALTHOUGH THE POOL AND SPA ARE not physically connected, they still share a water-circulation system. Visually, the pool, spa, and landscape are united through the repetition of circular design elements, including the round dish that aids in the flow of water between the spa and pool.

Custom Jets

HEAT AND HYDRAULICS make a hot tub or spa inviting, whether you're just looking to relax or are seeking a therapeutic massage. Today's spas come with elaborate jet systems—often dozens of jets, strategically placed for a neck-to-toe body massage. Many newer models enable you to control the jets individually, adjusting the flow or pressure for optimum comfort.

▼ THIS PORTABLE SPA IS PLACED ON A DECK WHERE
it is easily accessible year-round. Before placing a spa on a deck or porch, make sure structural beams are reinforced for the extra load.

▲ ALTHOUGH THIS SPA IS ADJACENT TO AND INTEGRATED into the shape of the pool, the circulation systems are separate. Separate systems are more efficient if the pool is not heated or is closed for much of the year.

▶ THIS SPA IS SET WITHIN THE POOL'S BOUNDARY AND slightly below the water level of the pool so the homeowners can use a single automatic pool cover. Covering a spa when it is not in use reduces heat loss and evaporation.

◄ PREFABRICATED SPAS OFFER comfortable, anatomically designed seating arrangements. The homeowners cleverly integrated this spa into the rugged landscape by adding a raised stone deck and wall, along with an arbor and ample plantings.

Energy Efficiency

HEATERS are a part of every spa system, and optional heaters can extend your season in the swimming pool. Heaters, however, can also run up your utility bill. Many solar heating systems are available, and all can help decrease your utility costs. When designing a pool, keep in mind that a shallow pool heats up more quickly than a deep pool, and that pools can be positioned for maximum sun exposure. If a pool site is exposed to winds, install windbreaks to reduce both water evaporation and wind chill.

◄ THIS SPA WAS PLACED IN AN OPEN AREA BETWEEN THE main house and guesthouse and screened with ornamental grasses for privacy. It offers excellent star-gazing potential.

Enclosing the Pool

Fences or walls surrounding a swimming pool are required in most towns. Even if local building codes don't require them, most homeowners' insurance policies do, as a solid wall or fence that can't be easily scaled will discourage trespassers and prevent unsupervised children from entering a pool. Although 4-foot-high fence requirements are common, a taller enclosure provides the greatest deterrent. In rural locations, where fences may not be required, an impenetrable hedge may satisfy your security needs. Fences, walls, and hedges, however, are more than just barriers. They can improve your sense of privacy, screen undesirable views, provide a solid backdrop for plantings, and surround a pool with warmth and character. A well-crafted wall or fence can greatly enhance the value of your property—especially if softened by attractive vines or used in combination with hedges.

▲ A FENCE OR WALL THAT SURROUNDS A POOL FOR security should be at least 4 ft. high, measured from the outside perimeter. Check local building codes for height requirements of pool fences.

▶ TWO BOUNDARY FENCES SURROUND this pool. The first fence runs the periphery of the property, and the second encloses the pool. The space between the fences provides pets and young children with plenty of room to play and assures parents that access to the pool and the street is secure.

▲ THE HOUSE SERVES AS ONE SIDE OF THIS pool enclosure. It is best to check local building codes before building a pool enclosure—some local ordinances specify that a fence must completely separate a pool from the house.

◄ THE RHYTHM OF HORIZONTAL LINES AND contrasting cutout shapes on this masonry wall complement the architecture of the house. The openings offer glimpses of the natural beauty of the landscape beyond without sacrificing privacy.

WALLS AND FENCES

▲ THE DARK RED PAINT AND ARCHED WOODEN GATE IN THIS MASONRY WALL DRAW the eye to the far end of the pool and backyard when viewed from the house and patio.

◀ USE GATES AND DOORWAYS TO FRAME enticing views of the pool or surrounding landscape. The iron gates of this entry frame the classical column at the pool's edge. Centering an architectural element in a doorway focuses the eye and signals to visitors that they are entering a soothing, orderly environment.

▲ GROWING VINES ALONG FENCES OR ARBORS IS AN EFFECTIVE WAY TO SOFTEN ALL THE HARD SURFACES COMMONLY found around a pool. An arbor tops this solid-wood fence, providing sturdy support for a climbing wisteria. The slatted roof creates dappled light and allows the air to circulate.

▲ MAKE SURE THAT POOL GATES CLOSE AND LATCH automatically so small children don't wander through doors accidentally left open. Some local building codes require the installation of gate alarms and periphery sensors around the pool area.

Playing It Safe

THE BEST POOL WALLS AND FENCES are high, smooth, and virtually impossible to scale. Although many local building codes may only require a 4-ft. wall or fence, the ideal height for a secure pool enclosure is 6 to 8 ft. Eliminate potential footholds, and close the gaps between fence pickets. Remove any nearby trees or objects that could aid someone trying to climb your fence, and make sure that gates both close and lock on their own. For extra safety, install gate and perimeter alarm systems to frighten off possible trespassers.

◄ THIS INGENIOUS FENCE DESIGN FILLS many needs. It meets security standards, screens nearby houses, and keeps overzealous deer from entering the yard. The lower half serves as a bench, and the upper half supports climbing vines. Copper caps on the finials protect the wood from weather damage while adding a decorative touch.

◄ LOW-MAINTENANCE METAL fencing is readily available, affordable, and easy to install. Many manufacturers offer finishes that do not have to be painted, and multiple styles are available to provide an elegant alternative to the chain-link fencing commonly found around a pool.

▶ THIS TALL MASONRY WALL IS positioned at the end of the pool for privacy; it screens the pool from the neighbor's view. Vine-covered chain-link fencing placed on a lower grade along the property's periphery meets the homeowner's security needs.

◀ SMOOTH, SOLID FENCING IS HARD TO SCALE, SO IT'S IDEAL FOR AROUND A POOL.
Although a standard dog-eared privacy fence would do the job, the curved profile and attractive posts of this painted fence add a decorative element to the landscape.

▲ TALL, METAL SECURITY FENCING IS PLACED DISCRETELY AROUND THE PERIPHERY of this property. Landscaping makes the fence almost invisible from the house and pool.

HEDGES

▲ HEDGES ALONE MAY NOT SATISFY LOCAL BUILDING CODES, BUT THEY ENHANCE A poolside setting and offer excellent screening. This hedge effectively hides a fence, which keeps young children and pets from entering the pool area unsupervised.

▲ TWO POSTS FLANKED BY DENSE, lush hedges support a decorative iron gate that leads into the pool area. The dark hedges offer an excellent backdrop for seasonal plantings.

▼ THE LONG HEDGES WORK IN UNISON WITH GATES, FENCES AND A POOLHOUSE to create a sense of enclosure around this pool. The wall of greenery behind the poolhouse increases privacy and offers a solid backdrop for the pool garden.

◄ THOUGH SCREENING IS MOST OFTEN used to hide a pool from view, it is also used to mask unwanted views from the pool. This long, low hedge screens the driveway from view. Because the driveway is a low, flat surface, a higher hedge was not needed.

Lighting for Safety and Pleasure

LIGHTING IS ESSENTIAL AROUND A POOL. It not only extends the hours you can spend around the pool, but also makes the pool a safer place after dark. Lighting plays another role, too—that of creating mood and an inviting environment. With the right lighting, you may find that evenings are the most delightful time around the pool. Three major types of poolside lighting are available: General lighting of the pool deck and passageways allows you to move about safely after dark. Underwater lighting enables nighttime swimming and creates special effects in the pool. Accent lighting in the garden, on structures, uplighting trees, or highlighting special architectural features adds atmosphere to any poolside setting.

▲ PATH LIGHTS ILLUMINATE THE STEPS AND THIS POOL DECK. WALL LAMPS AND TABLE CANDLES PROVIDE A MIX OF FUNCTIONAL and romantic lighting on the covered patio. Though these path lights are wired for electricity, wireless solar lights can be added easily to existing poolscapes.

► THE LIGHTING AROUND THIS POOL IS layered to be soft and welcoming. Underwater lights allow the homeowners to swim after dark. Uplights placed at ground level accent the pergola and container plantings. Built-in sidelights make the steps safe for passage. And finally, indoor lights call attention to the poolhouse.

▼ UPLIGHTS ADD DRAMA TO THE landscape by highlighting the sculptural qualities of tree trunks and by casting lacy shadows on the walls of the house. Down-lights provide general lighting for the deck and seating areas.

Fiber Optics Shed New Light on Pools

FIBER OPTIC LIGHTING is a safe and versatile option for illuminating pools. Instead of carrying an electric current, the lines that run to under-water fixtures carry only fibers of light. Fiber optic lighting also offers more design flexibility, because it is available in a wide range of styles and colors and can be used to create special effects—such as a kaleido-scope of changing colors or a rim of light beneath the pool's coping. Most existing pool lights can be retrofitted with fiber optic lighting.

▶ GENERAL LIGHTING, AS WELL AS "borrowed light" from the house's interior, brightens the gathering area. Uplights add drama to the setting by highlighting the tree branches overhead.

▼ UPLIGHTS, DOWNLIGHTS, PATH LIGHTS, house lights, and pool lights work together to create an inviting after-dark environment. When illuminated, the house is reflected in the pool.

▲ SMALL PATH LIGHTS ACCENT LOW PLANTINGS AND illuminate pathways around this pool. Fiber optic lighting in the pool gives the water a subtle glow.

◄ THESE HOMEOWNERS TOOK A SIMPLE YET EFFECTIVE approach to lighting. Coach lamps were placed near the home's doors, a single underwater light placed in the deep end of the pool to illuminate the water, and a couple of path lights keep the steps safe. The light from the interior of the house also spills over into the pool area.

Kids' Play Spaces

Under the right conditions, children can entertain themselves for hours. It helps to provide a variety of play spaces, as the interests of young minds can shift quickly. A lawn (it doesn't have to be large) for running around, kicking balls, and playing games is essential. A play structure with mix-and-match elements for climbing, sliding, and swinging can provide years of enjoyment and help improve coordination. A fort, playhouse, or tree house offers a fun, safe place in which to escape and engage the imagination. And kid-sized tables and chairs are ideal for quiet activities such as board games, tea parties, and art projects. All play areas benefit from a soft, cushioning layer of mulch or sand—especially around play structures or rough-and-tumble play spaces.

▼ CAREFUL ATTENTION TO LANDSCAPING makes this backyard a desirable destination for kids and adults alike. A play structure and small lawn are tucked neatly alongside a garden, while a curving path doubles as garden access and a tricycle path.

▲ KIDS NEED A PLACE TO UNWIND after rough-and-tumble activities, engage in quiet games, munch on afternoon snacks, or simply visit with friends. This colorfully shaded kids-size picnic table fits the bill perfectly as a space kids can call their own.

◄ SANDBOXES ARE FAVORITE play spaces for young children. This one was built from wood with a flat edge for seating and filled with play sand—a fine-grain sand that (unlike coarse builders' sand) has been filtered and cleaned and will not stain clothing.

▶ SIMULATED ROCK-CLIMBING WALLS are not limited to outdoor adventure stores. Children love the experience, so a low climbing wall with strong, closely placed hand- and footholds is ideal for backyard playgrounds. This one is approximately 4 ft. high and sits atop a soft pad of mulch.

▲ A CHALLENGING SITE doesn't have to limit activities. This custom-designed play structure takes advantage of a steeply sloping lot that has been terraced for improved accessibility. A slide from the sheltered lookout tower makes it easy for kids to reach the lower level.

◀ THERE ARE SEVERAL WAYS to go from the lower terrace back to the upper level. Children enjoy climbing this ladder or rescaling the slide, but parents tend to prefer steps, which are built at either end of the terrace.

Exploring Nature with Children

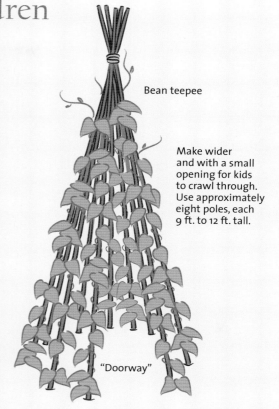

Bean teepee

Make wider and with a small opening for kids to crawl through. Use approximately eight poles, each 9 ft. to 12 ft. tall.

"Doorway"

BACKYARDS ARE THE PERFECT PLACE for children to learn about nature, whether through gardening or by creating a wildlife habitat for birds, toads, and butterflies.

Small gardens featuring giant flowers, easy-to-grow edibles, fuzzy foliage, and plants that attract butterflies can be planted and tended by children. For added interest, consider the following kid-friendly ideas: Grow beans up poles to form a teepee; create a corn or sunflower house by planting in a square and leaving a gap for the door; train a row of willow twigs into a living tunnel.

Pint-sized gardening tools are available to help with the task, and kids can have fun creating their own scarecrows each season. Older children may enjoy building a small greenhouse from salvaged supplies.

Backyard habitats provide food, water, cover, and safe places for small wildlife to raise their young. Trees and shrubs with nuts and fruit, as well as annuals and perennials with edible seed heads or nectar, will attract birds and butterflies. Shallow ponds are ideal for goldfish and for attracting toads. Birds will flock to birdfeeders, birdbaths, and birdhouses in any backyard. Even butterfly houses, bat houses, and toad houses will be occupied by guests in due time.

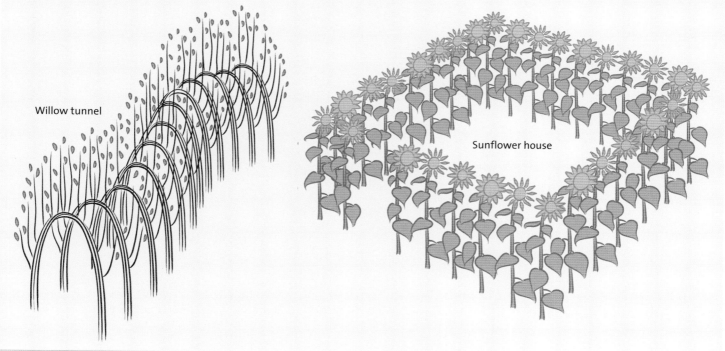

Willow tunnel

Sunflower house

▲ KIDS LOVE TO PLAY this handyman's version of a musical instrument, which is located beneath a tree house. Long bolts with oversized nuts were mounted on a swivel so that they could be used to strike the hollow copper pipes of varying lengths.

▶ A THICK, CUSHIONING LAYER of mulch provides a soft landing surface beneath this homemade backyard play structure, which features a fort, swings, tire swing, hammock, and slide. At least 6 in. to 8 in. of mulch is essential; some experts recommend 10 in. to 12 in.

▲ MUCH OF THE PLAYGROUND EQUIPMENT sold today is available in modular units, making it adaptable for varied budgets and kids of different ages. This one features a variety of climbing, sliding, swinging, and sitting elements to encourage a combination of quiet, athletic, and adventurous activities.

◄ IT'S NOT EXACTLY A TREE HOUSE, but the tree makes going down this slide more exciting and is a space-saving solution in a small backyard. The slide is attached to a small wooden platform for support and can be easily removed when the children outgrow it.

▲ TREE HOUSES CAN BE BUILT in a tree, around a tree, between trees, or on posts. This one is perched atop three sturdy limbs and features board-and-batten construction with a shingled, gable roof. The colorful paint job adds a sense of whimsy.

◄ THINGS ARE SLIGHTLY ASKEW in this brightly painted storybook playhouse. Surrounded by large-leaved hollyhocks and a flower-filled window box, it is a safe, convenient, and inviting play space that sparks the imagination of young children.

▲ A FEW OUNCES OF CREATIVITY can transform a garden shed into a magical playhouse. Painted shutters, window boxes, foundation plantings, and a faux chimney make this pint-sized place look like home. Tucked into a corner of the property, it doesn't overwhelm the backyard.

Creative Play Spaces

PLAY STRUCTURES DON'T HAVE TO BREAK THE BUDGET. A little imagination goes a long way when it comes to creative play spaces for young minds. Build a small platform for an outdoor stage or construct a puppet theater from plywood. Design an obstacle course that requires climbing a small tree, scrambling over a log, crawling beneath a hedge, and jumping over a puddle. Hang a tire swing from a strong tree limb with heavy-gauge rope. Pitch a tent for backyard sleepovers. Keep chalk handy for drawing on sidewalks or a recycled slate slab. Get your kids involved in coming up with ideas for the added benefit of sharpening creative thinking skills.

◄ BEING IN THE TREETOPS changes the way in which the world is viewed— both literally and figuratively speaking. This open-air deck offers kids a squirrel's-eye view of the backyard, while the garden swing gives parents or care-givers a place to relax nearby.

▼ THIS SCALED-DOWN VERSION of a shed is just the right size to lure young children down the garden path. By positioning it in the midst of a garden, children are afforded a unique oppor-tunity to observe and interact with nature.

▲ THIS UNIQUE TIRE SWING offers a new twist on an old theme. Strips of recycled tire rubber were ingeniously reassembled to create a swinging horse and then hung from a sturdy limb with heavy-duty rope.

▲ UPSTAIRS, DOWNSTAIRS, AND UP on the roof—this custom-built tree house (actually built on sturdy posts) offers a variety of indoor and outdoor places for keeping an eye on the neighborhood or escaping for a little privacy.

Game Areas

GAMES AREN'T JUST FOR THE YOUNG. They're also for the young at heart. In fact, they are a great way for families to spend more time together, as structured activities will often interest even the most independent teenagers. A small lawn planted with a tough turf grass is ideal for tag, croquet, softball, or volleyball. Other sports—such as horseshoes, shuffleboard, bocce ball, tennis, and basketball—require courts. Modular, suspended flooring, which is safer on the joints than concrete or asphalt, is now available in various court sizes suitable for backyard installation. Practicing on a backyard putting green is a sure way to improve a golf handicap, while billiard and table tennis equipment now come in waterproof models that are ideal for patios and pool decks. Paved areas for skateboarding, rollerblading, and roller hockey are also increasing in popularity. And a comfortable table and chairs are perfect for playing cards and board games.

▶ MOST BACKYARD PUTTING GREENS are made from low-maintenance artificial turf and come in a range of sizes and shapes. This one has been beautifully landscaped with boulders, naturalistic plantings, and even a waterfall.

▼ DINING TABLES CAN DO double duty as game tables on a porch, patio, or deck. Located beneath the shelter of a screened porch, this one is ideal for sunny or rainy day activities. Games can be stored nearby in a chest or cabinet.

◄ THIS BOCCE COURT is an eye-catching gathering space in a formal landscape (especially when viewed through this granite sculpture). The court itself is sunken, edged in cut stone, and filled with crushed gravel. It is surrounded by a tree-lined avenue, along with cast-stone benches.

▲ A RECTANGULAR AREA was carved out of this sloping backyard to create a flat game area. Although it is currently being used for croquet, it is also an appropriate shape and size for badminton, volleyball, and children's games like capture the flag.

► POOL TABLES ARE NOW AVAILABLE in waterproof outdoor models. This pool table was placed on a sunken game terrace located between the house and a broader terrace used for dining and entertaining. It's a favorite spot for the family teenagers.

▼ DESIGNED MORE FOR CONTEMPLATION than recreation, mazes and labyrinths provide a walking meditation for adults. Children also find them mesmerizing. This labyrinth was created by laying paths flush with the lawn. Mazes—in which you can't see where you are— are designed with hedge-lined paths.

◄ TABLE TENNIS IS A GOOD SPORT for the patio or terrace. Although this game table is weather resistant, its useful life can be extended by folding it up and rolling it under a nearby eave when not in use or if wet weather is in the forecast.

▲ CHILDREN LOVE TO BOUNCE (and parents love the extra energy it burns off)! Adding protective netting along the edges of this trampoline improves its safety and gives the parents peace of mind. Even with safety netting, however, children should be supervised when playing on a trampoline.

Playing It Safe

BACKYARD GAMES ARE ONLY FUN **if** nobody gets hurt. Game lawns should be flat and free from obstructions. Lawns and courts—in fact, any play spaces—should be placed away from fireplaces, grills, outdoor furniture, hard landscape surfaces, and fragile plantings. Activities that involve balls are best played away from windows and outdoor cooking areas. Play sets and swings need a thick layer of bark mulch, recycled rubber mulch, or play sand beneath them to create a soft landing surface. Also be sure to provide adequate lighting, as evenings are a favorite time for outdoor games and activities.

▲ GENEROUS LAWNS ARE THE MOST versatile recreational spaces in any yard. For safety and enjoyment, they should be level and free of stones, tree roots, and holes. This one is used for a variety of activities, from croquet to touch football to games of tag.

▶ THIS SMALL LAWN is just large enough for a child's game of soccer. Tough turf grasses such as perennial ryegrass, tall fescue, and St. Augustine grass are essential for recreational lawns that get trampled by feet on a day-to-day basis.

◄ THE DRIVEWAY IS STILL the most popular place to locate a basketball goal, but this home court is unique because it features built-in benches along the sidelines. Also, because the goal is attached to an arbor, the ball will not get stuck on the roof.

▲ ALTHOUGH THIS OUTDOOR CHESS SET is more for show than recreation, guests at parties have been known to engage in a not-so-serious game using these life-sized players. Lighter-weight, oversized models—which are designed for play—are also commercially available.

◄ KAYAKING, CANOEING, PADDLE BOAT-ING, and rowing are excellent forms of exercise for those fortunate enough to live near the water. These boats have been pulled up on a permanent dock that has been built from rot-resistant ipé, a tropical hardwood, at the edge of the patio.

Open-Air Showers

FOR MANY, AN OUTDOOR SHOWER CONJURES UP MEMORIES of the beach and rinsing the sand from feet and swimsuits before heading back into the house. But outdoor showers can also be part of an urban setting, providing a place to hose off your gardening clogs or even the dog.

Outdoor showers are a practical addition near a swimming pool, outside the back door, or just beyond the master bathroom. They can be built into a house wall or as separate units in the landscape, or they may be portable units hooked up to a garden hose. Unless they are used just for rinsing off or are built in a secluded location, outdoor showers need partial screening. (Total enclosure spoils the experience!) During the design process, provisions should be made for water access and adequate drainage. Towel bars, bath mats, and benches for clothing are much-appreciated amenities.

▶ INSTALLING A SHOWER against an exterior house wall offers an easy and affordable way to tap into water lines. This one is located just beyond the master bathroom and is used for washing off after a swim in the nearby lake or a soak in the spa.

▲ WHEN OUTDOOR SHOWERS ARE USED FOR BATHING, an enclosure built with rot-resistant, exterior-grade wood offers privacy. Benches, ledges, and hooks offer convenient spots to set down towels, hang swimsuits and clothing, or stash bathing necessities. Bath mats located just beyond the shower are also appreciated.

◄ SINCE THIS SHOWER IS USED FOR RINSING OFF before and after soaking in an in-ground spa, rather than for bathing outdoors, an enclosure was not necessary. The shower is tucked into a hedge to screen the wooden structure from view.

Portable Showers

An outdoor shower doesn't have to be fancy or expensive—particularly if your goal is simply to rinse off after a swim in the pool or soak in the spa. Several inexpensive portable models that hook up to garden hoses are now commercially available. And with a little ingenuity, a homemade model can be constructed in an afternoon by using a showerhead, a faucet, a few pipes and connectors, and some kind of a stand.

▲ SINCE OUTDOOR SHOWERING is a warm-weather activity, the plumbing for this shower is kept simple. It consists of exposed pipes and hoses connected to an outdoor spigot that can be easily disconnected and drained before cold weather sets in.

▲ A PORTABLE SHOWER IS SITUATED at the corner of a deck next to a movable spa. It connects easily to a garden hose, but a faucet knob is provided on the shower post for convenience. A shower curtain can be pulled for privacy.

▲ FOR THOSE WHO PREFER hot baths to showers, an outdoor tub is the ultimate luxury in relaxation. In this novel setup, dense landscaping provides screening from neighboring properties, and the stone wall offers a place to set soap, towels, and a change of clothes.

▲ THIS PORCH SHOWER features copper wall panels, naturally rot-resistant cedar posts, and ipé (tropical hardwood) caps and decking. Decking is spaced to allow water to fall into a galvanized drain pan, where it is carried off to a dry well in the woods.

Outdoor Décor

As the concept of outdoor living spaces has evolved over the past decade, exterior décor has followed suit. Outdoor rooms are being given the same design considerations as interior spaces, and the structural and decorative elements available to outfit them offer the same level of style and comfort that indoor rooms boast.

While garden structures are generally considered to be strictly utilitarian, they can also set the overall tone of an outdoor room by creating privacy, adding swaths of color and texture, and signifying a distinctive style. Water features, furniture, decorative accessories, and lighting build on this theme, making spaces not only more functional but also more comfortable, personal, and inviting.

Decorative elements can be chosen to match indoor décor, creating a sense of unity and flow between interior and exterior spaces. Or they may be selected to create an entirely different kind of space that distinctly separates it from the house. Many homeowners prefer to tie outdoor spaces to the garden, emphasizing natural materials in their choice of furnishings, water features, and decorative accents. The great thing about designing an outdoor room is that the sky is your limit. As long as furnishings can weather the elements, just about anything goes.

◀ MEXICAN TILE AND ARIZONA FLAGSTONE enrich this colorful southwestern courtyard, with both the tile colors and flagstone echoed in the table and chair cushions. The fountain masks neighborhood noise, adding to the serene setting.

Outdoor Structures

Fences, retaining walls, gates, paths, and arbors are often referred to as the "bones" of the landscape. Like walls in a house, they give shape to an outdoor space. And as the most dominant elements in any landscape, structures can also define its personality. Think of them as the walls, floors, ceilings, and doorways of your outdoor room.

It is often possible to identify the location or style of an outdoor room based on the design and materials of the structures alone. Adobe walls signify a southwestern courtyard as readily as a stacked-fieldstone wall does a New England landscape. Painted pickets are as at home around a cottage as glass blocks and metal are outside a modern residence. So taking cues from the architecture of your home and the indigenous landscape is an important first step in designing structures for your outdoor room.

▼ THE SIMPLICITY OF THE WHITE STUCCO WALLS allows this handcrafted teak gate to take center stage. The wall also serves as an effective backdrop for the plantings that mark the entrance to this garden room.

◀ OUTDOOR FLOORS ARE THE CANVAS for this artist, who creates detailed pebble mosaics from different-colored river cobbles by laying them in concrete before it hardens. It makes a sturdy, decorative surface for patios, terraces, and paths.

▼ THIS RUSTIC, HAND-HEWN GATE and arch overflow with character and old-time charm, blending right in with the rural setting. It is casual and inviting and sets the tone for a relaxed after-noon spent outdoors.

Gates with Personality

GATES—ESPECIALLY THOSE SEEN FROM THE STREET—make a strong first impression, so consider constructing something special. Most carpenters welcome the opportunity to show off their skills on a unique entry gate, and a local artist could design a one-of-a-kind gate just right for your home.

▲ THIS GATE FEATURES a unique thatched roof and carved door, setting the tone for the Asian-style garden beyond. The broom placed outside of the doorway is said to ward off evil spirits. It is placed bristles-up for good luck.

▼ A DECORATIVE, WROUGHT-IRON GATE is anchored to two stacked-stone posts, creating a formal but welcoming entry. Occasionally, such decorative gates can be found in home stores and catalogs. They can also be custom designed and fabricated by local artisans for a one-of-a-kind look.

▲ DECK RAILINGS, NEWEL POSTS, and finials can be custom designed to add character to any deck, stoop, or steps. This railing features unusual and colorful tile-mosaic finials made by the homeowner as an afternoon project.

Planting Pockets Soften Hard Surfaces

ONE OF THE EASIEST WAYS to soften the hard surfaces in a landscape is to encourage plants to grow in the cracks and crevices of a dry-laid retaining wall, patio floor, or path. Many creeping plants such as thyme, Corsican mint, and blue star creeper will grow in surprisingly tiny crevices between pavers if they are planted when small. Many herbs, along with plants that grow from seed or spore, such as corydalis and ferns, will make themselves at home in a retaining wall.

Larger planting pockets, in which a few stones have been removed and the soil has been amended with coarse sand or organic matter, can accommodate larger plants. In a sunny location, choose from heat- and drought-tolerant plants such as Mediterranean herbs and succulents for best results. Shady planting pockets can accommodate a wide range of small- to moderate-sized plants.

▲ DRY-STACKED STONE WALLS are attractive on their own, yet they can be further enhanced by planting some of the pockets between the stones. This one, located on a shady site, is filled with ferns. Herbs and succulents would be appropriate for a sunny site.

► GATES THAT CAN BE LOOKED THROUGH define boundaries yet encourage passersby to slow down and take a peak inside. The spindles on this handcrafted copper gate have been designed in the form of cattails, appropriately calling attention to the water garden just inside the courtyard.

▼ AN OPEN GATE is a sign of welcome. This one, with its bright yellow paint and widely spaced pickets, is especially cheerful and inviting. The straw hat adds a personal touch—expressing a warm and friendly invitation.

◄ LANDSCAPE STRUCTURES SUCH AS FENCES and gates play a strong role in setting the style and atmosphere of outdoor living spaces. This painted fence with playful cutouts creates a casual, lighthearted tone for activities that take place in this backyard.

▼ AN OUTDOOR ROOM with one or two carefully chosen objects can make a stronger statement than an outdoor room filled with decorative items. Here, the simplicity of paving materials and plantings allows the sculpture to shine and the distinctive arbor to define boundaries while maintaining an open feel.

Water Features

WATER IS MESMERIZING. It gives life to landscapes and outdoor living spaces and draws a crowd like a magnet. Whether a fish pond reflecting the autumn sky, the soft gurgling of a bubbling urn on a patio, or the energizing splash of a spa cascading into a swimming pool, water does more to create atmosphere in an outdoor room than perhaps any other element. It also has the unique ability to mask neighborhood noise.

Water features can be a significant component in an overall landscape plan or an easy addition to any deck, patio, porch, or garden. Ponds and waterfalls may require some basic construction skills, but it takes little more than a few inexpensive supplies and a couple of hours to create a container water garden or tabletop fountain. Many water features even come ready-made—just fill them with water and plug them into the nearest electrical outlet.

▼ THIS CARVED-STONE CONTAINER fills with water from the bamboo spout and then overflows into a basin located beneath the washed river stones. From there, a submersible pump recycles the water back through the bamboo spout. Hiding the bamboo in the foliage adds to the water feature's intrigue.

▲ THIS DECK FEELS MORE LIKE A DOCK because it overhangs the pond—which also gives the impression that the pond is larger than it really is. A pump was used to carry water to the dramatic cascade that spills over the wall, creating a special focal point.

◄ A CERAMIC BOWL, not to mention the birds of paradise plants, attracts feathered friends as well as the attention of passersby. The bowl also adds a sculptural element to the garden, and the crisp blue color complements nearby flowers.

▼ IT'S NOT EXACTLY a tabletop water feature, but water does flow into this striking stone table, which offers seating for six or more and is built into a retaining wall. Bottles of wine are often placed in the center of the table, where they are kept chilled by the water.

▲ A STEEP CITY LOT features a sunken courtyard outside a lower-level master bedroom. To bring the space to life, the hillside was terraced and planted, and a tiered waterfall of urns laid on their side was added to create a soothing, unique setting.

▶ THIS MANMADE, recirculating water-fall looks like a natural part of the land-scape because it features a single type of stone, carries an appropriate amount of water, discreetly hides the water source, and is softened along the edges by lush plantings.

◀ THE SOUND OF TRICKLING WATER, along with a hollow knocking (when the bamboo fills with water and tips over), emanates from this Japanese "deer scarer," or *Shishi-Odoshi*. Although once used to scare wild animals from rice patties, they more commonly appear in ornamental gardens today.

Musical Waterworks

DRIP, SPLASH, SLOSH, GURGLE, TRICKLE—just think of all the words used to describe the sound of water. Armed with a basic understanding of how water makes sound, plus a little trial and error, it's possible to create a symphony of sounds with water features.

To achieve the desired tone, try adjusting the volume of water, the distance that it falls, and the surface over which it falls. A rule of thumb: The greater the volume of water and the greater the distance it falls, the louder the sound it makes. Whether the water tumbles over a rough surface or falls directly into a pool of water also changes its character. Of course, sometimes it's the serenity of still water we cherish the most.

◀ A BUBBLING URN adds sound, movement, and a vertical accent to this round fishpond. The plants soften the hard surfaces, tie the water feature into the surrounding garden, and provide shade for the fish.

► THIS BUBBLING FOUNTAIN is self-contained in a stone basin. By stacking the stones, this water feature, along with the striking ornamental grass, adds an upright element to a narrow lot, making it feel more spacious. Landscape lighting helps it make a dramatic statement at night.

▲ SIMPLE YET ELEGANT, this wall fountain features a cast-concrete raven waterspout and copper basin. Water flows from the basin to the fountain through one copper pipe; the other pipe hides the electrical cord, which runs to a small pump.

► SIMPLE STONE BASINS—or deceptively realistic, faux-stone basins, as shown here—make excellent birdbaths and are especially suitable for a naturalistic setting. This one is surrounded by blue star creeper and serves as a surprise element in a flagstone patio.

Taking Cues from Nature

WHEN PLACING NATURALISTIC WATER FEATURES in the landscape, it's helpful to glean ideas and inspiration from the natural world. Ponds, for instance, should be situated in a low area rather than atop a hill. And the edge of naturalistic ponds should be irregular and ideally edged with a combination of half-buried stone and natural plantings that run beyond the water's edge and into the water. Waterfalls and cascades require high vantage points in a landscape so that the water has someplace to fall. Streams should meander, not run in straight lines.

Contradicting these basic principles results in a nature-inspired water feature with an unnatural appearance.

Formal and contemporary water features, however, offer considerably more freedom when it comes to design and placement. Fountains and reflecting pools can be placed in courtyards, on patios, on a lawn, or in the garden. Small water features, such as bowls and basins, bubbling stones and urns, or container water gardens, can be tucked almost anywhere in a landscape.

▲ WATER LILIES ARE JUST BEGINNING to put on their summer show in this man-made, but naturalistic, pond. Other plants, which add contrasting textures and shapes to the water garden, include water lettuce, iris, water hyacinth, cannas, and sedges.

▶ THE WINDING COURSE and varied ledge heights of this man-made water feature make it look natural. The stream gently drops into a small pool, where a pump carries water back up to a carefully hidden stream head.

▼ EVEN IN WINTER, before the perennials have filled in, this bubbling granite stone draws the homeowner outdoors. It provides year-round structure in the garden and is enhanced by the surrounding tile work, which leads visually to the fountain as a central point in the courtyard.

◄ ANY CONTAINER THAT HOLDS WATER can be used to create a water garden. This large ceramic pot was placed in the garden to hold water lilies. Because the pot has a dark interior, it reflects its surroundings—in this case, colorful foliage plants.

▲ RAISED FISHPONDS can be built on a patio with materials that either match or contrast with the paving surface. By matching the brick, this pond blends in subtly with its surroundings, helping to create a soothing environment.

◄ FOUNTAINS COME IN ALL shapes and sizes. Some, like this copper frog, even provide a touch of whimsy. This fountain was placed in a shallow pool and connected to an inexpensive, submersible pump that runs on 110 voltage.

◀ AN ELEGANT TIERED FOUNTAIN like this one can be made at home. You just need a series of pedestals and basins, a small pump, and a pool into which the water can collect before recirculating. This one spills into a channel built into the deck.

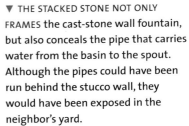

▼ THE STACKED STONE NOT ONLY FRAMES the cast-stone wall fountain, but also conceals the pipe that carries water from the basin to the spout. Although the pipes could have been run behind the stucco wall, they would have been exposed in the neighbor's yard.

▲ THIS MOSS-COVERED STATUARY FOUNTAIN looks as if it has been around for years but it's new. To speed up the aging process of new statuary, spray the basin with a mixture of water and buttermilk, then rub some moss over the surface. The spores should germinate quickly.

Easy, Affordable Water Features

Any container that holds water is fair game for a water feature. Simple or decorative birdbaths can anchor a border. Bowls, basins, pots, troughs, and barrels can be filled with water, moisture-loving plants (perched on bricks), and a few goldfish.

Water features of all sizes can benefit from the addition of a small fountain that runs on a fist-sized, submersible pump. Freestanding or tabletop fountains simply need to be filled with water and plugged into a nearby outlet. Just be sure that plugs and cords are designed for outdoor use and that outlets are covered and GFCI rated for safety.

▲ REFLECTING POOLS—still pools without fountains, streams, waterfalls, or cascades—are common elements in serene gardens like this one. They feature dark gray or black interiors, which easily reflect the sky, trees, and nearby buildings.

Fashionable Outdoor Furniture

OUTDOOR FURNITURE HAS COME A LONG WAY from the plastic
lawn chairs of old. As exterior furnishings have become an
increasingly hot commodity, manufacturers have developed
an impressive array of new materials and styles in price ranges to suit
any budget.

While the climate and your personal tastes figure into the decision-
making process, understanding how a space will be used—whether for
dining, conversation, or sunning—is the most important factor. It's also
important to know how many people will likely gather at a time. A cozy
bistro table may suit a romantic dinner for two, but an extension table
with folding chairs offers flexibility for larger groups.

Portability is also a plus outdoors. Medium-weight furniture can be
easily rearranged into varied conversation groupings to suit different
gatherings. Where harsh weather necessitates moving furniture indoors
for winter, lighter-weight chairs that can be folded or stacked make the
job much easier.

◄ COLORFUL SEAT
CUSHIONS both soften
these wrought-iron
chairs (physically and
visually) and color
coordinate with the
asters and purple
fountain grass in
the surrounding gar-
den. The dark, airy
wrought iron recedes
visually, allowing the
garden to remain
center stage.

◀ WICKER HAS LONG BEEN USED outdoors, but the new faux-wicker, which is made from woven resin on a powder-coated steel base, wears much better and lasts much longer, resisting water, ultraviolet rays, mold, mildew, stains, and sagging.

▲ THIS UNIQUE, HANDCRAFTED WOODEN BENCH is right at home in the arid, southwestern landscape. Despite its intricate paint job, it's safe from the sun and infrequent showers thanks to the adequate shelter of the portico. The same is true for the handwoven rug.

► THIS ONE-OF-A-KIND BENCH was placed beneath an aging apple tree not so much as a place to sit but as a way to convey a sense of serenity. It marks the entrance to a fragrant garden, where visitors are encouraged to stroll about slowly and deliberately.

▲ WHY CHOOSE PLAIN CHAIRS when there are so many decorative styles to pick from? These Adirondack-style chairs are given a tropical twist with their palm-tree cutouts. Painted to match the shutters and flooring, they lend a sense of unity to this front porch.

▲ USING THE LAWN instead of a more formal patio or deck for this seating area produces an inviting, naturalistic aesthetic; the tall plantings offer an organic wall, creating a sense of privacy. The log-cabin-style chairs and well-worn table are light enough to be easily moved when it's time to cut the grass.

Weather-Worthy Fabrics

STANDARD UPHOLSTERY CUSHIONS AND FABRICS don't wear well outdoors. Outdoor cushions must be quick drying and mildew resistant. Likewise, fabrics should be quick drying and treated for UV, mildew, and stain resistance. The most common outdoor fabrics are solution-dyed acrylic and vinyl-encapsulated mesh. Both come in a wide range of colors and patterns for easy styling and color coordination.

For longevity, store cushions indoors during winter, spot-cleaning fabrics with mild soap and warm water. To remove mildew, spray on a solution of 1 cup bleach, 2 cups mild detergent, and 1 gallon of water. Allow the solution to soak in, then rinse thoroughly. For tough stains, use a fabric stain remover.

▲ OUTDOOR FURNITURE STYLES are just as distinctive as their indoor cousins. The only difference is that outdoor furniture must withstand harsh weather and more casual treatment. The curved profile, deep cushions, and glossy, protective finish of these pieces suit the formality of the architecture.

► THESE CLASSIC FRONT-PORCH ROCKERS are a southern favorite. Although few rockers are weather resistant, they are ideally suited to covered areas such as porches and sunrooms. Choose from natural, stained, and painted finishes with wooden or woven seats.

▼ SOME FURNITURE WORKS INDOORS AND OUT, such as this painted-metal and ceramic bistro table and chairs. It would look equally at home in a kitchen, sunroom, porch, or patio. An occasional sanding and a fresh coat of paint will keep it looking great for years.

◄ A SUMPTUOUS, ELEGANT SOFA like this one offers a stylish alternative to deck chairs, and its bright color makes a dramatic statement against the landscape. Just make sure any outdoor sofas feature quick-drying cushions designed to resist water, fading, mildew, and stains.

Wear and Care of Outdoor Furniture

SEASONAL CARE GREATLY EXTENDS the life-span of outdoor furniture. At least once a year, clean wood furniture with trisodium phosphate (TSP). Teak and cedar can weather naturally, but other woods need a fresh coat of varnish, stain, or paint.

Wash metal furniture with mild soap and warm water, and apply paste wax to prevent corrosion. Also rinse resin and plastic furniture. If stained or mildewed, wash with 1 cup of bleach, 2 cups of detergent, and 1 gallon of water. Gently machine-wash and hang-dry fabric seats, placing them on their frames while still damp to prevent shrinking. Vacuum outdoor wicker, then clean it with soapy water and apply a protective paste wax finish.

▲ THOSE WITH A KNACK for building things can make their own patio furniture. This stylized version of an Adirondack chair is a perfect example of great-looking, handcrafted furniture. A matching chest, which holds seat cushions but also works as an occasional table, stands nearby.

◄ THIS ARBOR PROVIDES a hanging structure for the hammock, as well as affording partial shade—a more comfortable arrangement in strong summer sun. It was tucked along one side of the backyard where young children playing on the lawn could be easily watched.

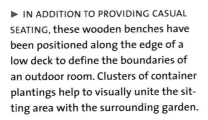 TEAK IS A CLASSIC IN THE GARDEN. It adapts to many design styles, such as the contemporary set shown here, is sturdy and long lasting, and weathers to a beautiful gray patina with little or no care. It can even be left outdoors in winter (although it will last longer if stored indoors).

▶ IN ADDITION TO PROVIDING CASUAL SEATING, these wooden benches have been positioned along the edge of a low deck to define the boundaries of an outdoor room. Clusters of container plantings help to visually unite the sitting area with the surrounding garden.

◀ MIXING AND MATCHING OUTDOOR FURNITURE can form a sophisticated design style, just as it does indoors. In addition to wrought-iron and teak furniture, this outdoor room features both cushioned and noncushioned seating. It's just enough variety to make the space interesting without appearing busy.

▶ YARD SALES AND FLEA MARKETS are excellent sources for one-of-a-kind, mix-and-match furnishings. Old pieces in rough condition can be rescued and given new life, as was done with the old-fashioned folding chair shown here, with sandpaper, a fresh coat of paint, and a little creativity.

Simplify for a Soothing Setting

WHEN IT COMES TO OUTDOOR DÉCOR, **just about anything goes. But keep in mind that instead of being framed by flat walls, floors, and ceilings, most outdoor rooms feature few flat surfaces and may be dominated by plant foliage, fences, arbors, detailed paving materials, and an ever-changing sky. So the surroundings are, visually speaking, busy to begin with.**

If your goal is to create an energizing environment, go all out with bright colors and splashy designs. But if a soothing setting is preferred, keep the design simple. Limit the number of decorative objects in any one area, and select furnishings and accoutrements with natural finishes and clean lines. Also, limit the number of accent colors—whether in plantings or hard landscaping materials. Pastels, shades of white or gray, and harmonious (versus contrasting) colors tend to work best. And restricting the color palette to shades of green can be especially pleasing outdoors because it is such a natural choice.

▲ THIS SMALL DECK was designed as a getaway for one. The clean lines and natural materials of the teak chair, the gray walls, and the minimal decorative accents in the surroundings create a calm, soothing environment.

BUILT-IN SEATING

▶ A RUGGED BENCH is also a retaining wall. Because it's made from large stones and small boulders, it blends in unobtrusively with the surrounding landscape and provides a quiet spot to sit and enjoy the nearby pond.

▲ THIS PATIO FEATURES a mix of built-in and freestanding furnishings—all brightly colored to evoke a tropical theme emphasized by the plantings of palms, cannas, glory bush, and agapanthus. The tabletop lanterns add an appropriate finishing touch, with their blue panes picking up the color of nearby planters.

▲ THE FREESTANDING BENCH AND TABLE on this rooftop were designed to look like built-in furniture and make the most of limited space. They are solidly built—a significant consideration for rooftop locations where strong winds can be a challenge.

◄ ALTHOUGH THIS MAY NOT BE the most comfortable chair in the garden, it is the most unusual. Made entirely from recycled concrete, it offers a point of conversation if not a place to pause briefly while touring or working in the garden.

Accents and Accessories

STRUCTURES MAY DEFINE AN OUTDOOR SPACE and even signify its overall style, but accents and accessories give it personality. Such elements are limited only by your imagination and their ability to weather outdoor conditions. Objects can be mounted on house and garden walls, positioned in borders as focal points, clustered on tables or the ground, or hung from tree limbs and arbors.

With or without plants, containers are the most obvious choice for outdoor accents. Statuary and sculpture are also favorites, while weather-resistant pillows can add color and comfort to an outdoor room. Curtains and blinds create visual warmth while keeping inclement weather at bay, and market umbrellas and awnings do double duty as practical yet aesthetic enhancements. Even waterproof rugs are now available to help make patios look and feel more like rooms designed expressly for living. As long as the accessories express your style and complement their surroundings, you can't go wrong.

▲ MOSAICS, WHICH ARE CREATED BY PRESSING broken tiles and china into just-poured concrete, are easy to make and add a touch of color to any landscape. Here, bits and pieces of broken china and tile were transformed into a unique birdbath.

◀ DECORATIVE OBJECTS, especially when combined with architectural elements, can effectively carry out a decorating theme. Here, everything has an Asian flair—from the evergreen plantings and bamboo fence to the lantern and wall-mounted fish carving.

▲ FINDING NEW USES for common objects adds an element of surprise to any outdoor setting. This old garden bench has been put into service as a coffee table. Its faded paint echoes the colors in the pillows and flowers.

▲ THIS PORTICO USES A MIDDLE-EASTERN MOTIF to create a dramatic room without breaking the bank. The furnishings can easily be found at garage sales and discount stores and then dressed up with colorful fabrics. The hanging lantern, stars, and birdcage offer rich detail without a big price tag.

◀ MIRRORS ARE AN UNEXPECTED ELEMENT in outdoor rooms, but they can be used effectively to reflect light into shaded spaces and make a small space feel larger—just like indoors. These are flanked by curtains made from shade cloth, which is used to protect tender plants.

◀ IT'S A SNAP TO ADD A TOUCH of country charm, even in an urban setting. This homeowner transformed a small outdoor area with a faded board fence, old garden tools, a rustic bench, pots of ivy, casual paving, and ruffled pillows.

Art in the Garden

ART TAKES MANY FORMS IN THE GARDEN—sculpture, statuary, found objects, architectural accents, folk art, and even mobiles. All help define the personality of an outdoor room or landscape and can bring a space to life. The key to using art successfully rests in its placement. Employ a favorite piece as a focal point at the end of a straight path or as a surprise element along a curving one, against a fence that can be viewed from indoors, as an anchor for a perennial border, or hanging from an arbor as an unexpected overhead object.

Landscapes are also excellent places to showcase collections of art. Try clustering several pieces to create a vignette, space them with a sense of rhythm to draw you through a garden, or showcase a single dominant piece within each visual space or outdoor room. This gives the art a sense of purpose and helps to avoid a haphazard, cluttered look that could detract from a collection's beauty.

Just make sure elements chosen as outdoor art can handle the elements. Porous objects may crack with winter's freeze-thaw cycle, metals may rust, some ceramic glazes may flake or fade from sun exposure, and wood may rot, especially if it's in contact with the ground.

▲ USING FAMILIAR OBJECTS in unfamiliar ways creates drama. Gazing globes are usually placed singly in the garden, atop a metal stand. Here, a whole row of gazing globes placed on the ground provides an unexpected counterpoint to the stark, yet dramatic, tree trunks.

CONTAINER PLANTINGS

◀ THIS GATHERING OF POTS makes a strong impression because the pots are staged on different levels. In addition to using a tiered plant stand, pots can be placed on steps, upturned empty pots, bricks, or outdoor furniture.

▼ PATHS, PATIOS, DECKS, AND PORCHES are excellent places to group container plantings. Cluster them along curves, at corners, next to posts, or adjacent to steps. This backyard arrangement exemplifies the visual interest that is created when the size of the clusters are varied.

▲ THESE CONTAINERS WERE PLANTED individually and clustered to create a striking grouping. They work well together because the succulents contrast in texture, shape, size, and color. If plants that looked similar had been chosen, the composition would have been much less interesting.

Quench Container Thirst

THE GREATEST CHALLENGE WITH GROWING PLANTS in pots is keeping them watered. It's not unusual for them to need water twice a day in hot, dry weather. To minimize watering needs, start with large pots. They hold more soil and won't dry out as quickly as small pots. Mix 2 parts potting soil with 1 part compost to improve water retention. Water-absorbing crystals, used modestly, can also help.

And finally, connect pots to a drip irrigation system with an automatic timer, especially if there are lots of pots in a concentrated area such as a deck or patio. That way, plants get watered even when you go on vacation.

▲ MATCHING CONTAINER PLANTINGS can be used to call attention to passageways—a door to the house, steps onto a deck, an arbor, or a path that leads around the side of a house. These planters filled with ferns mark the entrance to a garden path.

◀ THIS COLORFUL WINDOW BOX, which has been filled with easy-to-grow annuals, can be enjoyed from indoors and out. By using annuals, the planting can be changed several times during the year to keep it looking fresh and to reflect the changing seasons.

▼ BY PLACING MULTIPLE PLANTS in a single large pot, a self-contained garden is formed for this poolside patio. This planting works particularly well because it combines both upright and trailing plants. Within a matter of weeks, the sprawling petunias will obscure the planter altogether.

▲ CONTAINER PLANTINGS CREATE THE ILLUSION of walls around this small backyard patio, while a driftwood container hosts a living sculpture against the house wall and a tall container filled with trailing greenery softens the house corner. Together, they make a cozy setting for outdoor dining.

◀ WINDOW BOXES CAN BE HUNG on the walls of porches, decks, and patios to create focal points; this one is positioned near the front door where it makes a dramatic statement. Foliage plants were used to add a splash of color.

Supporting Players

Y ou've mulled over the design possibilities of the front of the house—the entry, the lawn, and the lighting. But have you given any thought to supporting structures like gates and garages, fences and driveways? All of these elements are large and prominent features that can make or break the overall appearance of your home.

Fences and gates are important for privacy and security reasons, but because they cover so much of the landscape, it's essential that they be attractive as well as secure. To make a fence more of a handsome feature, consider adding highly decorative garden structures like arbors and pergolas.

Driveways and garages are often a given: For better or worse, they come with the house. But a garage or driveway can undergo a makeover as easily as any other part of your home or yard. Any garage will look better if the details on or around the door harmonize with exterior elements elsewhere on the house. And a driveway can be completely transformed just by upgrading paving materials.

◀ THIS GRAND ENTRANCE enclosed by a gated stone wall makes use of three of the most common materials for driveways—asphalt, stone pavers, and gravel. Stone pavers are an attractive feature and they serve a practical purpose: They keep gravel from washing out onto the asphalt.

Fences, Walls, and Gates

FENCES AND WALLS serve many purposes. They define property lines, create privacy, keep wandering animals in or out, even shore up a terrace or a sloped yard. But from the standpoint of curb appeal, they should always be attractive as well as functional.

Materials for fences include wood, vinyl, and metal. The most durable and attractive woods for fences include cedar and redwood. But no matter which material you choose, keep in mind that in a front yard, a fence should be "friendly." That means you want it to be open enough to see through. Place the gate so that it allows for easy passage into the front yard; in most cases, it should open onto the path to the front door.

Walls are usually made of stone or brick. These sturdy constructions suggest a degree of substance and permanence in addition to their other roles. To keep a stone or brick wall neighborly, make sure it's not much taller than waist high.

▲ A GATE DOESN'T necessarily need to match its fence to be charming. This substantial double-door gate in natural wood resembles a double entry door. The Arts-and-Crafts–style "windows" in each panel make the doors seem friendly and approachable to guests and visitors.

◄ NOTHING SETS OFF A LANDSCAPE like a stone wall. Because each stone is laid individually, a stone wall can be tailored to fit any yard. Unlike mortared stone walls, drystacked stone walls have a natural appearance. Because they require masonry skills to carefully set each stone without mortar, however, they tend to be costly.

▲ A WHITE PICKET FENCE is the perfect enclosure for older or more traditional homes. This fence clearly outlines property borders, but it's also charming and easy to see through. It also features an unusual turnstile gate. To add a splash of color, plant climbing roses or clematis at the base of the arbor posts.

◄ PLANK FENCING is an attractive solution for an area where you want privacy. Usually made of cedar, plank fences are built in ready-made sections that attach to pressure-treated posts dug on site. In this fence, the top sections include latticework to allow some light and visibility into the yard.

FENCES AND GATES

▲ EVEN IF ITS DESIGN allows visitors to peak inside, a fence can still provide privacy. Although this gray and white fence is composed of wide and narrow slats with narrow gaps between them, it's difficult to see inside without making an effort.

▶ IN THE RIGHT SETTING, a simple post fence and gate can look just right. This airy post-and-rail fence is made of inexpensive and easily available cedar. Its open style defines the property line without interfering with the spectacular view.

► THE CENTERPIECE of any fence is the front gate. The posts on either side of the gate should be a little larger than those on the rest of the fence so that the gate stands out. To call even more attention to the gate, add decorative elements to the posts like these ball finials.

▲ A PLANK GATE gives even the flimsiest fence a sense of substance. Hanging lanterns on either side of this scalloped-shape gate with a delightful overhead arbor ensure a safe and warm welcome well after the sun goes down.

◄ SINCE THE PATTERN of a picket fence is naturally repetitious, do something decorative to set the gate apart. Here, the heights of the gate pickets are varied, making the entrance easier for visitors to see and enter through.

Picket Fence Patterns

AN INVITING PICKET FENCE is a time-honored enclosure for a small front yard or garden. Picket fences are made of flat, evenly spaced slats nailed top and bottom to horizontal railings. Like most wood fences, picket fences can be constructed in sections that attach to posts mounted in the ground.

Picket tops are easy to cut into countless shapes to make the fence more ornamental; diamond point, round, and acorn are some of the most common designs. The slats also lend themselves to decorative cutouts, such as notches, circles, or squares.

Although vinyl is available, wood is still the most attractive material for picket fences. Choose a good-quality, water-resistant wood such as cedar, and take care that your pickets don't touch the ground. The posts, which will be in contact with the ground, should be pressure-treated to prevent rot. Keep a solid-wood fence sealed or painted, and it will reward you with years of service.

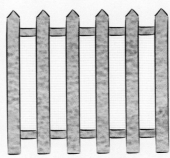
Diamond point

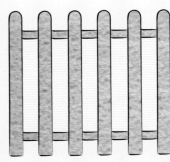
Round

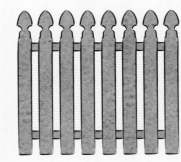
Acorn

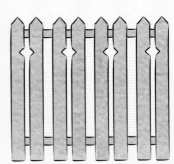
Diamond points with cutouts

► A FORMAL GATE is the perfect opening statement for a formal house. Centering the gate in line with the front door gives this property a complete sense of balance. To create a well-designed gate, look to details on your house. These gate posts are modeled on the columns around the front door.

◄ SOMETIMES TWO FENCES are better than one. A low stone wall provides support for a sloping yard, while a picket fence adds the security of a front gate. By painting the picket fence white, the homeowners brightened up their home by calling attention to the color of the house trim.

► AN ADOBE HOUSE all but calls out for an adobe fence. While this enclosure is especially tall to provide privacy, a lower wall could work in a more expansive setting. A bold arch clearly marks the entrance to the interior courtyard, which is visible through the novel metal gate.

▲ A WIDE GATE can make a high brick or stone wall less intimidating. This wood-plank gate fits snugly under an unusual brick archway that ties the gate in to the fence, spanning a double-width opening. The gate can be left invitingly ajar or securely locked.

WALLS

▲ WALLS CAN BE of almost any height. This low stone wall encloses a lush courtyard planted with shrubs, a spreading evergreen, and a flowering tree. The wall is low enough to make a cozy spot for wandering without losing contact with the yard beyond.

◄ WALLS FINISH OFF NEATLY with pillars that are slightly higher than the wall itself. This pair is topped with planters and provides crisp definition between a gravel driveway and the flagstone path leading to the house.

▶ A PATH LEADING THROUGH a stone and mortar wall crosses a dry stone bed, or arroyo, meant to resemble a river. While the tan and gray stones in the wall suggest the solidity of land, the blue stones in the arroyo suggest water.

◀ TIERED WALLS—one high, one low—come to the rescue of a house that's both close to the sidewalk and high above it. The space between the two walls makes an ideal planting bed. Painting the walls white helps set off colors and textures in the plantings.

PERGOLAS

▲ AN ARBOR IS A SMALL VERSION of a pergola that arches over a door or gate. Although arbors are largely decorative, they can also support growing plants. This arbor encourages a rose-bush covered with pink blossoms to twine around its exposed rafters.

▲ A PERGOLA—a flat-roofed, openwork structure—is an ideal way to add pizzazz to a garden gate. The open rafters let in air and sunlight but are sturdy enough to support climbing vines that create a restful, shady space underneath.

► EVEN THOUGH PERGOLAS are typically open at the top, you can also include a covered section to provide extra shade or shelter. A sitting area at the juncture of this walkway and courtyard provides a good spot to escape a sudden shower or await a ride.

▲ IF YOU WANT TO CREATE SHADE along a walk but don't want to cover the area with a roof, build an extended pergola. This one is supported by rounded columns and screened by latticework with circular openings.

▲ THIS UNUSUALLY ORNATE FENCE incorporates two pergolas into its design—one over the gate and another over an interior walkway. The rafters that lie flat on top of the pergola repeat the pattern of the square, slender spindles grouped together in twos and threes in the fence, tying the two structures together.

Driveways

WHETHER YOUR DRIVEWAY IS LONG OR SHORT, it should be an asset to your house. Just like a walkway, a driveway usually needs maintenance and a refreshing of the surface material every few years. Cracked concrete, grass sprouting through asphalt, and gravel that is patchy in places can all severely compromise your home's appearance.

A driveway should be functional, too—at least 11 ft. wide and long enough for a driver to pull in safely from the street or to back out. Give some thought to the path your drive takes on its way to the house or garage: Straight or gently curving is usually best, with a flared entry where the drive meets the street. Consider, too, whether you want to include room for more than one parking space as part of the driveway or a turnaround space somewhere along the drive.

Finally, if your lot is small, don't overdo it: Keep the size of the driveway in scale with the house.

▶ LONG APPROACHES can be charming ones. If your drive is especially long, try to tie it to the landscape that it passes through. Edge it with shrubs or trees, or allow grass to grow between the tire tracks, for example.

▲ STONE PAVERS MAKE A DURABLE, easy-care surface for a driveway or parking area. Be sure to choose pavers that are intended for exterior use and that can bear weight.

◄ A CURVING DRIVEWAY will allow your house to shine upon approach, rather than calling attention to the garage. If you have enough space, place the parking area behind your house. This will allow you to create a driveway that doesn't threaten to visually dominate your home.

MATERIALS FOR DRIVEWAYS

◄ IF YOUR GARAGE IS ATTRACTIVE, the drive itself needn't stand out. It's important to keep the surface of the driveway in good repair, though: A few cracks or weeds sprouting through the asphalt can undermine the appearance of the rest of your property.

▼ EXPANSES OF BLACK ASPHALT can be visually overwhelming if they are in the front of a house. This asphalt drive, however, unifies the house and the garage. To further tie the driveway to the nearby architecture, the owner wisely chose a paint scheme that harmonizes with the shade of the asphalt.

▲ A CHIPPED-STONE DRIVEWAY next to a flagstone walk has a pebbly texture that complements the shingled exterior of this house. The drive is also edged with low pavers, which help keep the loose material where it belongs, rather than in the yard.

Driveway Paving Materials

DRIVEWAYS CAN BE PAVED with almost any material that drains well and stays more or less in place. The most durable materials include asphalt, concrete, pavers, and gravel, a medium that can vary from pea size to small stones.

- ASPHALT is a petroleum byproduct that arrives as a ready-to-spread hot mix. The hot mix is compacted by heavy rollers to create a smooth surface that should wear for years. Asphalt works well in cooler climates (the black color absorbs heat and can speed up snow and ice melt). It's less popular in warmer climates, where it can soften and develop ruts or gouges when it's exposed to high temperatures.

- CONCRETE is a mixture of sand, gravel, and cement that's poured in place. The surface is smoothed or brushed before it cures. Able to withstand extreme heat, it's the paving material of choice in hot climates. Concrete can also be pigmented, giving you a range of color choices. It can be subjected to any number of decorative treatments before it's fully cured, including stamping or etching to create interesting patterns like faux brick or stone.

- PAVERS are man-made stones that resemble either stone or brick. Made of clay and other natural materials, they are engineered to resist cracking in all types of weather extremes including freeze/thaw cycles and dry heat. Pavers are more expensive than either asphalt or concrete and cost more to install because they are laid by hand in interlocking patterns. If you like the look, however, this durable material will last indefinitely.

- GRAVEL is the least expensive material for driveways. Made of crushed, chipped, or natural stone, it comes in various sizes and colors. Gravel works well in cold or hot climates, but it needs to be refreshed with new gravel fairly often, particularly if the gravel is especially small (pea gravel). To keep gravel where you want it, consider adding a section of pavers, concrete, or asphalt at the turn-in to the driveway and alongside the edges of the drive. This will help keep the gravel from jumping out of its bed into the street and yard.

◄ KEPT NEATLY IN CHECK by a low wall and mulched planting beds, this gravel driveway makes an attractive approach. Because it is porous and allows water to percolate through to the soil layer, gravel works well in areas where rainwater tends to pond or cause flooding.

▲ BRICK PAVERS OFFER A broad range of natural earth colors that make them a beautiful choice for a driveway. The bricks can be laid in just as many patterns as a brick path, too, from traditional running bond to basket weave.

▶ STONE PAVERS IN A LIGHT GRAY color are an excellent choice for a driveway with a slightly below-grade garage. While asphalt would also be a good choice, a loose material like gravel wouldn't work here because it would tend to spread into the garage.

◄ GRAVEL IS THE LEAST-EXPENSIVE paving material for driveways, but it needs frequent replenishing to keep the surface crisp and even. Edging the drive with a stone border can help keep the gravel in place and provide a barrier against creeping grass.

▲ THIS DRIVEWAY IS PAVED with a combination of materials. To handle the wear and tear of traffic, the owners put the most durable material on the tire tracks. They provided contrast by using gravel (a material, like grass, that drains well) as a supporting player.

◄ ASPHALT DRIVEWAYS are easy to install and last for many years. The material doesn't need an edge treatment and can be installed flush against a sidewalk, making it a good choice where easy accessibility is a factor.

▲ AN UNPAVED DRIVEWAY with grass growing between the tire tracks recalls a more relaxed era when cars were used less frequently. There's no rule that says you can't leave room for grass in a driveway, but you will have to cut it occasionally.

Matching Driveway to House Style

CHOOSE A MATERIAL FOR YOUR DRIVE that either complements some aspect of the house or contrasts with it in a pleasing way. For instance, brick pavers might seem like a natural choice for a red brick house, but the double whammy of brick drive and brick house might be overwhelming. A material of a different color—gray or black asphalt, light brown or gray gravel, or blue stone pavers—might give your drive just the lift it needs. Another trick is to match the color of the paving material to the color of the roof shingles, since there's a good chance the shingles already complement your home's exterior and provide a little contrast to the siding color.

◄ A BED OF STONE GRAVEL appears to flow like a river between stone embedded in the ground. The material is a good choice because it shares an affinity with both the natural landscape and the gray color of the roof.

▲ IF YOUR YARD is big enough to accommodate one, a circular driveway can be especially useful because it allows vehicles to safely reverse direction. Because circular drives cover so much territory, they work best in yards with enough room for a dedicated parking area separate from areas for play and relaxation.

◄ EDGING AN EXPANSE OF ASPHALT with stone pavers gives a drive-way a more permanent, finished look. The pavers gracefully mark the transition between the drive and the lawn. Since they are solid and stable, they also help prevent erosion at the edges of the asphalt.

Garages

ALMOST EVERY HOUSE seems to have a garage these days—with anywhere from one to three bays. Because garage bays tend to be wide and uniform in style, there's a danger that what many Americans regard as the ultimate necessity can overwhelm the appearance of an otherwise desirable house.

There are many ways to conceal or improve the appearance of a garage, even one with multiple bays. The design of the garage door, the placement of the garage within the façade, and well-chosen paint colors can make any garage better looking, if not exactly a thing of beauty. And if you are considering adding a garage as part of an addition or style makeover, by all means consider the design impact of this new structure with as much care as the rest of your home. A garage should complement a house, not dominate it.

▲ BECAUSE IT'S ON the lowest level, a townhouse garage tends to be less noticeable than other types of garages. The owner of this house further disguised its presence by adding a columned porch that doubles as the garage entry.

◄ TO MAKE AN ATTACHED GARAGE blend in with the rest of your house, paint it either the color of your house or the color of the house trim. Or add an accent that echoes the style of the home, like the arch over this garage door.

▲ A GARAGE THAT'S SET APART from the main house and matches it in style often has as much curb appeal as the house itself. This one is set behind the house, eliminating any possibility that it will appear overwhelming and visually dominate the nearby house.

► CARPORTS ARE A SHADY alternative to an enclosed garage in warmer climates, where sun and rain do more damage than ice and cold. A car parked outdoors is also more accessible. This area does double duty as a patio.

▼ TO MAKE THE MOST of the interior of a stand-alone garage, put the stairs to the second floor on the outside of the building. Nicely finished with a balustrade and capped posts, these include entry porches on the ground and second levels.

► SINCE A FREESTANDING GARAGE is as big as a small house, it makes sense to create finished space on the second floor. Options include space for an office, guest quarters, or an apartment for rental income.

◄ THESE SLIDING GARAGE DOORS are decorated with diagonal cross bars to form an attractive pattern. Upstairs, the builder has created a variation on the cross-bar theme by adding a decorative grid at right angles to a large window.

IN THE DETAILS

Hiding Garbage Cans

KEEP YOUR TRASH and recycling bins out of sight—behind the house or tucked away in the garage if possible. If the trash must be kept out front, disguise or hide it with a screen, small shed, or partially enclosed fence. While you can build your own screen with materials from a home supply or builder's store, be on the lookout for ready-made screens and kits, which can save you time and money.

▶ HIDE YOUR TRASH BARREL until pick-up day with a freestanding screen in teak or cypress. The latticework on this ready-made screen conceals the barrel, yet allows for plenty of ventilation.

▲ TUCK GARBAGE CANS away in a small storage shed. This one is finished with sturdy doors and locks, a must in areas where garbage-loving animals like raccoons are a problem.

► WHENEVER TWO OR MORE garage bays are grouped together, look for a way to break up the monotony. One time-honored method is to add architectural ornament: The curving cross-brace detail in this gable draws the eye away from the two bays but at the same time links both of them together.

▲ THE OWNERS OF THIS NEW shingled home came up with an inventive way to incorporate a double-bay garage without extensive blasting of the surrounding bedrock. The solution was to turn the garage at a 45-degree angle, which kept site costs in check.

A Garage Makeover

WHEN A NEW JERSEY couple purchased this tiny Cape, it was just big enough for two. Once a baby was due, however, the architect-owner began to think about the "bigger picture." A new garage was part of an expansion that more than tripled the size of the house. The owner kept the feel of the original Cape and transformed the cramped side entry into a larger breezeway that connects the house to the new garage.

The garage is linked to the remodeled house architecturally, with some important style differences that help keep it subordinate to the main house and also identify its function. The diagonal cross braces on the garage doors make it abundantly clear which part of the house is for cars and which is for people.

▲ AT 600 SQ. FT., this tiny Cape lacked a lot more than a garage before it was remodeled. The cramped side entry set back from the main part of the house, however, was the germ of an idea for a connecting breezeway to the new garage.

▲ ALTHOUGH THE ROOF PITCH on both the house and garage are closely matched, details in the top of the gables vary slightly: There are fish-scale shingles under the peak of the roof on the house, while a standing-seam tin detail appears on the garage.

◄ ALTHOUGH ALL THREE of these garage doors match and are arranged in a line, the interesting shapes of the surrounding stucco architecture provide some visual relief. The fact that one of the doors is slightly wider than the other two single-car doors beside it is another variation that keeps the garage from looking dull.

Credits

p. 125: Photo © Mark Samu, courtesy Hearst Specials.
p. 126: (top) Photo by Jeff Beneke, © The Taunton Press, Inc.; (bottom) Photo © Brian Vanden Brink, Photographer 2003, Architect: Jack Silverio, Lincolnville, ME.
p. 127: (top) Photo by Jeff Beneke, © The Taunton Press, Inc.; (bottom) Photo © 2003 carolynbates.com, Architect: Marcel Beaudin, South Burlington, VT, General contractor: George Hubbard, Hubbard Construction, Inc., Williston, VT.
p. 128: Photo © Brian Vanden Brink, Photographer 2003, Margo Jones, Architect, Greenfield, MA.
p. 129: (top) Photo © Brian Vanden Brink, Photographer 2003, Tony DiGregorio Architect, Damariscotta, ME; (bottom) Photo © Robert Perron, Photographer, Elena Kalman, Architect, Stamford, CT.
p. 130: (top) Photo courtesy California Redwood Association; (bottom) Photo © 2003 carolynbates.com, Jean Henshaw Design, Shelburne, VT.
p. 131: (top) Photo © Robert Perron, Photographer, Robert Knight Architects, Blue Hill, ME; (bottom) Photo by Roe Osborn, courtesy Fine Homebuilding, © The Taunton Press, Inc., Architect: Bryan Wilson, Block Island, RI.
p. 132: (top) Photo © Robert Perron, Photographer, Interior Design, Old Lyme, CT; (bottom) Photo © Robert Perron, Photographer.
p. 133: (top) Photo © Ken Gutmaker; (bottom) Photo by Charles Miller, courtesy *Fine Homebuilding,* © The Taunton Press, Inc.
p. 134: Photo © Robert Perron, Photographer, Paul Bailey Architect, New Haven, CT.
p. 135: (top) Photo © 2003 carolynbates.com, Cushman & Beckstrom Architecture and Planning, Inc., Stowe, VT; (bottom) Photo by Charles Bickford, courtesy *Fine Homebuilding,* © The Taunton Press, Inc., Architect: Charles Mueller, Centerbrook Architects, Essex, CT.
p. 136: Photo © 2003 carolynbates.com, Office of H. Keith Wagner, Landscape Architects, Burlington, VT.
p. 137: (top left) Photo © Brian Vanden Brink, Photographer 2003, Mark Hutker & Associates Architects, Vineyard Haven, MA; (right) Photo © Robert Perron, Photographer, Robert Knight Architects, Blue Hill, ME; (bottom left) Photo © Robert Perron, Photographer, Architect: J. P. Franzen, Southport, CT; Oliver Nurseries, Fairfield, CT.
p. 138: (top) Photo © Jessie Walker; (bottom) Photo © Robert Perron, Photographer, Architect: William Nowysz, Iowa City, IA.
p. 140: (top) Photo © Brian Vanden Brink, Photographer 2003, Winton Scott Architects, Portland, ME; (bottom) Photo © Robert Perron, Photographer, B&B Landscaping, Mystic, CT.
p. 141: (top) Photo © Brian Vanden Brink, Photographer 2003, Architect: Jack Silverio, Lincolnville, ME; (bottom) Photo © Robert Perron, Photographer, Ken Walden Landscape, ME.
p. 142: Photo by Charles Miller, courtesy Fine Homebuilding, © The Taunton Press, Inc., House + House Architects, San Francisco.
p. 143: (left) Photo © Robert Perron, Photographer.
p. 144: Photo © Brian Vanden Brink, Photographer 2003, Architect: Jack Silverio, Lincolnville, ME.
p. 145: (top) Photo © 2003 carolynbates.com, Design: Linda Vail, ASID, Vail Design Group, Colchester, VT (bottom) Photo © Brian Vanden Brink, Photographer 2003.
p. 146: Photo © Robert Perron, Photographer, Zak Landscape, CT.
p. 147: (top) Photo © Brian Vanden Brink, Photographer 2003, Architect: Peter Rose, Cambridge, MA; (bottom) Photo © 2003 carolynbates.com, Cushman & Beckstrom Architecture and Planning, Inc.
p. 148: (top) Photo by Charles Miller, courtesy Fine Homebuilding, © The Taunton Press, Inc., House + House Architects, San Francisco, CA; (bottom) Photo by Andy Engel, courtesy *Fine Homebuilding,* © The Taunton Press, Inc., Architect: Kevin McKenna, Columbia, MD.
p. 149: (top) Photo © Brian Vanden Brink, Photographer 2003, Architect: Lo Yi Chan, New York, NY; (bottom) Photo © Robert Perron, Photographer, Architect: Kagan Company, New Haven, CT.
p. 150: Photo © Brian Vanden Brink, Photographer 2003, Ron Forest Fences, Scarborough, ME.
p. 151: (top) Photo © Brian Vanden Brink, Photographer 2003, Mark Hutker & Associates, Architects, Vineyard Haven, MA (bottom) Photo © Brian Vanden Brink, Photographer 2003, Horiuchi & Solien Landscape Architects, Falmouth, MA.
p. 152: (left) Photo © Todd Caverly/Brian Vanden Brink Photographs, Whipple-Callender Architects, Portland, ME; (right) Photo © Robert Perron, Photographer, Eastern Timber Homes, Leverett, NH.
p. 153: (top) Photo © Jessie Walker; (bottom) Photo © Brian Vanden Brink, Photographer 2003.
p. 154: (top) Photo © Jessie Walker; (bottom) Photo © Mark Samu, courtesy Hearst Specials.
p. 155: Photo by David Ericson, courtesy Fine Homebuilding, © The Taunton Press, Inc., Architect: Patrick McClane, Richmond, VA.
p. 156: (left) Photo © Robert Perron, Photographer, Landscape: Anne Penniman, Essex, CT; (top right) Photo © 2003 carolynbates.com, Artist: Don Kjelleren, Charlotte, VT; (bottom right) Photo © Brian Vanden Brink, Photographer 2003, Horiuchi & Solien Landscape Architects, Falmouth, MA.
p. 157: Photo © Robert Perron, Photographer, Architect: Paul Bailey, New Haven, CT.
p. 158: (top left) Photo © Brian Vanden Brink, Photographer 2003, Centerbrook Architects, Essex, CT; (bottom right) Photo © Robert Perron, Photographer; (right) Photo © Mark Samu, Architect: Mojo Stumer AIA, Roslyn, NY.
p. 159: Photo © Robert Perron, Photographer, Landscape: Anne Penniman, Essex, CT.
p. 160: (top) Photo © Brian Vanden Brink, Photographer 2003, Architect: Roc Caivano, Bar Harbor, ME; (bottom) Photo © Robert Perron, Photographer, Landscape: Shep Butler, Thetford, VT.
p. 161: (top) Photo © davidduncanlivingston.com; (bottom) Photo © davidduncanlivingston.com.
p. 162: Photo © 2003 carolynbates.com, General contractor: Tom Clark, A. W. Clark Jr. & Son, Inc., Waitsfield, VT.
p. 163: (left) Photo © Steven House, Architect: House + House, San Francisco, CA; (top right) Photo © Robert Perron, Photographer, Architect: Don Watson, Troy, NY; (bottom right) Photo © Robert Perron, Photographer, Architect: Don Watson, Troy, NY.
p. 164: (top) Photo © Robert Perron, Photographer, Builder: Steve Cavanaugh, Hamden, CT; (bottom) Photo © Robert Perron, Photographer.
p. 165: (top) Photo © davidduncanlivingston.com; (bottom) Photo © Robert Perron, Photographer, Architect: Gisolfi Associates, Hastings on Hudson, NY.
p. 166: (top) Photo © 2003 carolynbates.com, General contractor: Tom Sheppard, Sheppard Custom Homes, Inc., Williston, VT; (bottom) Photo © davidduncanlivingston.com.
p. 167: Photo © davidduncanlivingston.com.
p. 168: Photo © Mark Samu, Architect: Mojo Stumer, AIA, Roslyn, NY.
p. 169: (top) Photo © davidduncanlivingston.com; (bottom) Photo © Mark Samu, Architect: Noelker & Hull Associates, Chambersburg, PA.
p. 170: (top) Photo © davidduncanlivingston.com; (bottom left) Photo © Robert Perron, Photographer, Landscape: Janet Cavanaugh, VT; (bottom right) Photo © david- duncanlivingston.com.
p. 171: Photo © Robert Perron, Photographer, Designer: Leslie Darroch, Branford, CT.
p. 172: Brian Vanden Brink, photo © 2005.
p. 173: left: Photo © Deidra Walpole.
p. 174: (top) Photo © Deidra Walpole; Design: Ruby Begonia Fine Gardens; (bottom) Photo © Lee Anne White; Design: Simmonds & Associates.
p. 175: Photo © Deidra Walpole; Design: Ruby Begonia Fine Gardens.
p. 176: Photos: © Lee Anne White; Designs: Desert Sage Builders.
p. 177: (top) Photo © Lee Anne White; Design: Linda Marr &Jackye Meinicke; (bottom) Photo © Deidra Walpole; Design: The Green Scene.
p. 178: Photo © Lee Anne White; Design: Four Dimensions Landscape.
p. 179: (left) Photo © Allan Mandell; Design: Milari Hare; (right) Photo © Lee Anne White; Design: Simmonds & Associates.
p. 180: (top) Photo © Lee Anne White; Design: JC Enterprise Services Inc.; (bottom) Photo © Lee Anne White.
p. 181: Photo courtesy Dacor.
p. 182: (top) Photo courtesy Dacor; (bottom) Photo © Allan Mandell; Design: Ron Wagner & Nani Waddoups.
p. 183: (top) Photo courtesy DACOR; (center) Photo © Lee Anne White; (bottom) Photo © Lee Anne White; Design: Betty Romberg.
p.184: Photo © Deidra Walpole; Design: The Green Scene.
p. 185: (left) Photo © Deidra Walpole; Design: Ruby Begonia Fine Gardens; (right) Photo © Lee Anne White; Design: Desert Sage Builders.
p. 186: (top) Photo © Deidra Walpole; Design: The Green Scene; (bottom) Photo © Deidra Walpole; Design: Mark David Levine Design Associates.
p. 187: Photo © Lee Anne White; Design: Colette Bullock.
p. 188: (top) Photo © Lee Anne White; Design: Michelle Derviss; (bottom) Photo © Lee Anne White; Design: Jim Harrington Garden Design.
p.189: Photo © Lee Anne White; Design: Linda Marr and Jackye Meinicke.
p. 190: (left) Photo courtesy Paul Faaborg/topgrill.com; (right) Photo © Lee Anne White; Design: Desert Sage Builders.
p. 191: (top) Photo © Lee Anne White; Design: JC Enterprise Services, Inc.; (bottom) Photo © Lee Anne White; Design: Bill Feinberg, Allied Kitchen & Bath.
p. 192: Photo: Brian Vanden Brink, photo © 2005; Design: Polhemus Savery Da Silva.
p. 193: (top & bottom) Photos Brian Vanden Brink, photo © 2005; Design: Mark Hutker & Associates Architects.
p. 194: (left) Brian Vanden Brink, photo © 2005; Design: Polhemus Savery Da Silva; (right) Photo © Allan Mandell; Design: Myrna Wright.
p. 195: (top) Photo © Tim Street-Porter; (bottom) Photo by Todd Meier, © The Taunton Press, Inc.; Design: Alan Franz.
p. 196: (left) Photo © Allan Mandell; Design: Linda Ernst; (top right) Photo © Lee Anne White; Design: JC Enterprise Services, Inc.; (bottom right) Photo © Lee Anne White; Design: Dan Cleveland.
p. 197: (top) Photo © Allan Mandell; Design: Pamela Burton; (bottom) Photo © Allan Mandell; Design: Les Bugajski.
p. 198: (left) Photo © Lee Anne White; Design: Four Dimensions; (right) Photo © Lee Anne White; Design: Michelle Derviss.
p. 199: (left) Photo © Allan Mandell; Design: Ron Wagner & Nani Waddoups; (right) Photo © Lee Anne White; Design: Richard McPherson.
p. 200: (top) Photo © Deidra Walpole; Design: Robert Marien; (bottom) Photo © Lee Anne White; Design: Colette Bullock.
p. 201: (left) Photo © Deidra Walpole; Design: Ruby Begonia Fine Gardens; (right) Photo © Deidra Walpole; Design: Flower to the People.
p. 202: Photo © J. Paul Moore; Design: The Porch Company.
p. 203: Brian Vanden Brink, photo © 2005.
p. 204: Brian Vanden Brink, photo © 2005; Design: Peter Breese.
p. 205: (top) Brian Vanden Brink, photo © 2005; Design: John Cole, architect; (bottom) Photo by Daniel S. Morrison, © The Taunton Press, Inc.; Design: Al Platt, architect.
p. 206: Photo © Tria Giovan.
p. 207: (left) Photo © J. Paul Moore; Design: The Porch Company; (right) Photo © Tria Giovan.
p. 208-209: Photos © J. Paul Moore; Designs: The Porch Company.
p. 210: (top) Photo © Tria Giovan; (bottom) Photo by Roe A. Osborn, © The Taunton Press, Inc.; Design: Paul DeGroot, architect.
p. 211: (top) Photo by Charles Bickford, © The Taunton Press, Inc.; Design: Sarah Susanka, architect; (bottom) Photo © Anne Gummerson Photography; Design: Hammond-Wilson Architects and Oehme, van Sweden Associates, landscape architects.
p. 212: (left) Brian Vanden Brink, photo © 2005; Design: Sally Weston, architect; (right) Photo © Tria Giovan.
p. 213: Brian Vanden Brink, photo © 2005.
p. 214: (left) Photo © J. Paul Moore; Design: The Porch Company; (right) Photo © Allan Mandell; Design: Duley Mahar.
p. 215: Photo © Allan Mandell; Design: Joyce Furman.
p. 216: (left) Brian Vanden Brink, photo © 2005; Design: Mark Hutker & Associates; (right) Brian Vanden Brink, photo © 2005.
p. 217: Photo © Allan Mandell.
p. 218: (left) Photo © Deidra Walpole; Design: Kennedy Landscape Design Associates; (right) Photo © Deidra Walpole; Design: Ruby Begonia Fine Gardens.
p. 219: (top) Photo © Dency Kane; Design: Don Morris & Harry White; (bottom) Photo © Deidra Walpole; Design: Mayita Donos Garden Design.
p. 220: (top) Photo © www.kenricephoto.com; (bottom) Photo: © Deidra Walpole; Design: Ruby Begonia Fine Gardens.
p. 221: Photo © Mark Turner; Design: Patricia & Robert Lundquist.
p. 222: (top) Photo © Jerry Pavia; (bottom) Photo © Deidra Walpole.
p. 223: Photo © Mark Turner; Design: Larry & Stephanie Feeney.
p. 224: Photo by Todd Meier, © The Taunton Press, Inc.; Design: Alan Franz.
p. 225: (top) Photo by Steve Aitken, © The Taunton Press, Inc.; Design: Jim Scott; (bottom) Brian Vanden Brink, photo © 2005; Design: Horiuchi & Sollen Landscape Architects.

p. 226: Photo © Tim Street-Porter.

p. 227: (top) Photo © Tim Street-Porter; Design: Tom Beeton; (bottom) Photo © Tim Street-Porter; Design: Page Marchese Norman.

p. 228: Photo © Tim Street-Porter; Design: Nancy Goslee Power.

p. 229: (top) Photo © 2005 Carolyn L. Bates/carolynbates.com; (bottom) Photo © Tim Street-Porter; Design: Page Marchese Norman.

p. 230: (top) Photo © Lee Anne White; Design: Desert Sage Builders; (bottom left) Photo © Lee Anne White; Design: Michelle Derviss; (bottom right) Photo © Lee Anne White; Design: David Thorne.

p. 231: Photo © Deidra Walpole; Design: Mayita Donos Garden Design.

p. 232: (top) Photo © www.kenricephoto.com; (bottom) Photo © Deidra Walpole; Design: New Lead Landscape Design.

p. 233: Photo © Lee Anne White.

p. 234: (top) Photo © Dency Kane; Design: Cathy Cullen; (bottom) Photo © Deidra Walpole; Design: Green Scene Landscape Design.

p. 235: (top) Photo © J. Paul Moore; Design: The Porch Company; (bottom) Photo © 2005 Carolyn L. Bates/carolynbates. com; Design: Catherine Clemens, Clemens and Associates, Inc.

p. 236: Photo © Jerry Pavia.

p. 237: (top) Photo © Jerry Pavia; (bottom left) Photo © Mark Turner; Design: Larry & Stephanie Feeney; (bottom right) Photo © 2005 Carolyn L. Bates/carolynbates.com; Design: Catherine Clemens, Clemens and Associates, Inc.

p. 238: (top) Photo © Deidra Walpole; Design: Green Scene Landscape Design; (bottom) Photo by Jennifer Brown, © The Taunton Press, Inc.; Design: Rosalind Reed.

p. 239: Photo © Tim Street-Porter; Design: Annie Kelly.

CHAPTER 8

p. 240: Photo © 2005 Carolyn L. Bates/carolynbates.com; Design: H. Keith Wagner, Wagner McCann Studio.

p. 241: left: Photo © Tria Giovan.

p. 242: Photo: © Tim Street-Porter.

p. 243 (top) Photo © John Glover/Positive Images, Design: Glen Fries, landscape architect.

p. 244: (top) Photo © davidduncanlivingston.com; (bottom) Photo: © Brian Vanden Brink, Photographer 2004, Design: Mark Hutker Associates, Architects.

p. 245: Photo: © Tim Street-Porter.

p. 246: Photo: © Lee Anne White, House and pool design: Bill Remick, Architect; (bottom) Photo: © Tim Street-Porter.

p. 247: Photo: © davidduncanlivingston.com.

p. 248: (top) Photo: © Roger Turk/Northlight Photography 2004; (bottom) Photo: © Barbara Bourne Photography, Design: Aquatic Technology.

p. 249: (top) Photo: © Tria Giovan, Design: Robert Norris, Architect; (bottom) Photo: © Andrew McKinney.

p. 250: (top) Photo: © Barbara Bourne Photography, Design: Aquatic Technology; (bottom): © Lee Anne White, Design: Leisure Living Pools.

p. 251: (top) Photo: © Lee Anne White, Design: Atlanta Pools, Inc., Cummings, GA; (bottom) Photo: © Lee Anne White, Design: Leisure Living Pools.

p. 252: (top) Photo: © Alan Mandell, Design: Hendrikus Schravenn, Issaquah, WA. (bottom) Photo © Lee Anne White, Landscape Design: Paula Refi, Stone Design: Mark Grubaugh.

p. 253: Photo: © Steve Silk.

p. 254: (top) Photo: © The Taunton Press, Inc., Design: John Donahue; (bottom) Photo: © Andrew McKinney, Design: Jack Chandler & Associates.

p. 255: top: Photo: © The Taunton Press, Inc., Design: John Donahue; (bottom) Photo: © Jerry Pavia Photography, Inc.

p. 256: (top) Photo: © Alan Mandell, Design: Clark Matschek, Portland, OR; (center) Photo: © Jerry Pavia Photography, Inc.; (bottom) Photo: © Jerry Pavia Photography, Inc.

p. 257: (top) Photo: © Karen Bussolini/Positive Images, Design: Tramontano & Rowe; (bottom) Photo: © Gay Bumgarner/Positive Images.

p. 258: Photo: © Roger Turk/Northlight Photography 2004.

p. 259: Photo: © Brian Vanden Brink, Photographer 2004, Location: Cape Cod, MA, Design: Perry Dean Rogers & Partners, Architects.

p. 260:(top) Photo: © Andrew McKinney, Design: Jack Chandler & Associates; (center) Photo: © Alan Mandell, Design: Pamela Burton, Santa Monica,CA; (bottom) Photo: © Dency Kane.

p. 261: Photo: © Brian Vanden Brink, Photographer 2004, Design: John Morris, Architect.

p. 262: Photo: © Lee Anne White, Design: Michelle Derviss.

p. 263: (top) Photo: © Lee Anne White; (bottom) Photo: © The Taunton Press, Inc.

p. 264: (top)Photo: © Jerry Pavia Photography, Inc.; (bottom) Photo: © Karen Bussolini/Positive Images, Design: Lisa Tamm, landscape architect.

p. 265: (top) Photo: © Karen Bussolini/Positive Images, Design: Johnsen Landscape & Pools, Mt. Kisco, NY; (bottom) Photo: © Tim Street-Porter.

p. 266:(top) Photo: © Karen Bussolini/Positive Images, Design: Johnsen Landscape & Pools, Mt. Kisco, NY; (bottom) Photo: © Gay Bumgarner/Positive Images.

p. 267: Photo: © The Taunton Press, Inc., Design: Connie Cross.

p. 268: (top) Photo: © Tim Street-Porter, Design: Tichenor & Thorpe; (bottom) Photo: © Tim Street-Porter.

p. 269: (top) Photo: © Karen Bussolini/Positive Images; (bottom) Photo: Tony Benner, courtesy Master Pools by Artistic Pools Inc., Atlanta, GA.

p. 270: (top) Photo courtesy Crestwood Pools, Charlotte, NC; (center & bottom) Photo courtesy National Spa & Pool Institute.

p. 271: Photo courtesy National Spa & Pool Institute.

p. 272: Photo:Tony Benner, courtesy Master Pools by Artistic Pools Inc., Atlanta, GA.

p. 273: (top) Photo: © Lee Anne White, Design: Ellis Lan Design; (bottom left) Photo: © Lee Anne White, Design: David Thorne, Landscape architect; (bottom right) Photo:Tony Benner, courtesy Master Pools by Artistic Pools Inc., Atlanta, GA.

p. 274: (top) Photo: © Jerry Pavia Photography, Inc.; (bottom) Photo: © Barbara Bourne Photography, Design: Aquatic Technology.

p. 275: (top) Photo: © Lee Anne White, Design: Richard McPherson, Landscape architect; (bottom) Photo: © Karen Bussolini/Positive Images, Design: Glenn Fries, Landscape architect.

p. 276: (top left) Photo: © Jerry Pavia Photography, Inc.; (top right) Photo: © Brian Vanden Brink, Photographer 2004, Design: Roc Caivano; (bottom) Photo: © Lee Anne White, Design: David Thorne, Landscape architect, Poolhouse: Bev Thorne, Architect.

p. 277: (top) Photo: © Barbara Bourne Photography, Design: Aquatic Technology, Landscape: GardenArt; (bottom) Photo: © Brian Vanden Brink, Photographer 2004, Design: Mark Hutker Associates, Architects.

p. 278: (top & bottom) Photo: © Brian Vanden Brink, Photographer 2004, Design: Horiuchi & Solien, Landscape architects.

p. 279: (top) Photo: © Brian Vanden Brink, Photographer 2004, Design: Ron Forest Fences; (bottom) Photo: © Tim Street-Porter.

p. 280: (top) Photo: © Lee Anne White, Design: Carrie Nimmer; (bottom) Photo: © Tria Giovan, Location: Palm Beach, FL.

p. 281: Photo: © davidduncanlivingston.com.

p. 282: Photo: © Dency Kane, Design: Richard Cohen and Jim Kutz, Amagansett, NY.

p. 283: (top) Photo: © Lee Anne White, Design: Michelle Derviss; (bottom) Photo: © Lee Anne White, Design: Leisure Living Pools.

p. 284: (top) Photo: © Karen Bussolini/Positive Images, Design: Johnsen Landscape & Pools, Mt. Kisco, NY; (bottom) Photo: © Lee Anne White.

p. 285: Photo: © Lee Anne White, Design: David Thorne, Landscape architect.

p. 286: (top right) Photo: © Brian Vanden Brink, Photographer 2004, Design: Horiuchi & Solien, Landscape architects; (top left) Photo: © Tria Giovan.

p. 287: (top) Photo: © Dency Kane; (bottom) Photo: © Dency Kane.

p. 288: Photo: © Barry Halkin.

p. 289: (top) Photo: © Barry Halkin; (bottom) Photo: © Brian Vanden Brink, Photographer 2004, Design: Payette & Associates, Architects.

p. 290: (top) Photo: © Brian Vanden Brink, Photographer 2004, Design: Perry Dean Rogers & Partners, Architects; (bottom) Photo: © Samu Studios, Inc., Design: Jim De Luca, A.I.A.

p. 291: (top) Photo: © Anne Gummerson Photography, Design: Jay Huyett/Studio Three Architects; (bottom) Photo: © Roger Turk/Northlight Photography 2004.

p. 292: Photo © Lee Anne White; Design: Michelle Derviss.

p. 293: (top) Photo © Lee Anne White; Design: JC Enterprise Services; (bottom) Photo © Lee Anne White; Design: Michelle Derviss.

p. 294 (all) Photo © Lee Anne White; Designs: Michelle Derviss.

p. 296 (left & right) Photo © Lee Anne White; Design: Jim Harrington Garden Design.

p. 297: (top) Photo © Deidra Walpole; Design: Ruby Begonia Fine Gardens; (bottom) Photo © Mark Turner; Design: Pat & Sienke Stevenson.

p. 298-299: Photos © Jerry Pavia.

p. 300: (top & bottom left) Photos © Jerry Pavia; (bottom right) Photo © Dency Kane.

p. 301: Photo © Jerry Pavia.

p. 302: Brian Vanden Brink, photo © 2005; Design: Horiuchi & Solien.

p. 303: (top) Photo © Alan & Linda Detrick; Design: cording Landscape Design; (bottom left) Brian Vanden Brink, photo © 2005; (bottom right) Photo © Deidra Walpole; Design: Chris Johnson.

p. 304: (top) Photo © Lee Anne White; Design: David Thorne; (bottom) Photo © Dency Kane; Design: Barbara Putnam.

p. 305: (top & bottom) Photos © Lee Anne White; Designs: JC Enterprise Services.

p. 306: (top) Photo © Lee Anne White; Design: David Thorne, landscape architect; (bottom) Photo © Lee Anne White; Design: Michelle Derviss.

p. 307: (left, top & bottom) Photos: © Lee Anne White; Designs: Simmonds & Associates; (right) Photo by Steve Aitken, © The Taunton Press, Inc.; Design: Jim Scott.

p. 308: Photo © Lee Anne White; Design: Simmonds & Associates.

p. 309: (left) Photo © Lee Anne White; Design: Michelle Derviss; (right) Photo © Tria Giovan.

p. 310: (top right): Photo by Andy Engel, © The Taunton Press, Inc.; Design: Ron Cascio; (bottom right) Photo © Allan Mandell; Design: Jeffery Bale; (left) Photo © Lee Anne White.

p. 311: Photo by Andy Engel, © The Taunton Press, Inc.

CHAPTER 9

p. 312: Photo © Lee Anne White; Design: Joan Lewis, Cathy Feser, & Ruben Gonzales.

p. 313: Photo left © Tim Street-Porter.

p. 314: Photo © Deidra Walpole.

p. 315: (left) Photo © Allan Mandell; Design: Des Kennedy; (right) Photo © Allan Mandell; Design: Joanne Fuller.

p. 316: Photo © Allan Mandell; Design: Ron Wagner and Nani Waddoups.

p. 317: (top left) Photo by Jennifer Benner, © The Taunton Press, Inc.; Design: Lucy Hardiman; (top right) Photo © Anne Gummerson Photography; Design: Nan Patternotte; (bottom) Photo © Deidra Walpole; Design: Hannah Carter.

p. 318: (left) Photo © Jerry Pavia; (right) Photo © Deidra Walpole.

p. 319: (top) Photo © Anne Gummerson Photography; Design: William Riggs; (bottom) Photo © Anne Gummerson Photography; Design: Sarah Schweizer, architect, and John Slater, landscape designer.

p. 320: (top) Photo © Deidra Walpole; Design: Hannah Carter; (bottom) Brian Vanden Brink, photo © 2005; Design: Robinson & Grisary, architects.

p. 321: (top) Photo © Tim Street-Porter; Design: Joseph Marek; (bottom) Photo by Steve Aitken,© The Taunton Press, Inc.; Design: Jim Scott.

p. 322: (left) Photo © Lee Anne White; Design: Jeni Webber; (right) Photo © Allan Mandell.

p. 323: (top) Photo © Allan Mandell; Design: Portland Japanese Garden; (bottom) Photo © Allan Mandell; Design: Michael Schultz.

p. 324: (top left) Photo © Lee Anne White; Design: Jeni Webber; (top right) Photo © Lee Anne White; Design: Richard McPherson; (bottom) Photo © Allan Mandell; Design: Berger Partnership.

p. 325: Brian Vanden Brink, photo © 2005; Design: John Morris, architect.

p. 326: (top) Photo © Alan & Linda Detrick; (bottom) Photo © Lee Anne White; Design: Joan Lewis, Cathy Feser, & Ruben Gonzales.

p. 327: (top left) Photo © Allan Mandell; Design: Linda Cochran; (right) Photo © Tria Giovan; (bottom) Photo © Dency Kane; Design: Martin Viette Nursery.

p. 328: (left) Photo © Alan & Linda Detrick; Design: Marlise Johnson; (top right) Photo © Alan & Linda Detrick; Design: Marshalwick Horticultural Society; (bottom) Photo © Deidra Walpole; Design: New Leaf Landscape Design.

p. 329: Photo © Anne Gummerson Photography; Design: Nan Patternotte.

p. 330: Photo © Allan Mandell; Design: Nancy Hammer.

p. 331: (left) Photo © Tria Giovan; (right) Photo © Lee Anne White.

p. 332: (top) Photo © Allan Mandell; Design: Barbara Blossom Ashmun; (bottom left) Photo © Lee Anne White; (bottom right) Photo © Mark Turner; Design: Christine Haulgren.

p. 333: Photo: Brian Vanden Brink, photo © 2005; Design: Weatherend Estate Furniture.

p. 334: (left) Photo © Allan Mandell; Design: Tom Hobbs; (top right) Photo © Allan Mandell; Design: Mike Snyder; (bottom) Photo © Tim Street-Porter.

p. 335: (left) Photo © Lee Anne White; Design: Michelle Derviss; (right) Photo © Tim Street-Porter.

p. 336: (top) Photo © Tria Giovan; (bottom) Photo © Allan Mandell; Design: Dotty & Jim Walters.

p. 337: (top left) Photo by Todd Meier, © The Taunton Press, Inc.; Design: James Woodel & Kimmy Tilley; (top right) Photo © Tim Street-Porter; (bottom) Brian Vanden Brink, photo © 2005; Design: Polhemus Savery DaSilva.

p. 338: (top) Photo © Dency Kane; Design: Richard Cohen & Jim Kutz; (bottom) Photo © Tim Street-Porter.

p. 339: (left) Photo © Allan Mandell; Design: Roger Raiche & David McCrory, Planet Horticulture; (right) Photo © Deidra Walpole.

p. 340: (top) Photo by Jennifer Brown, © The Taunton Press, Inc.; Design: Lucy Hardiman; (bottom) Photo © Tim Street-Porter.

p. 341: Photo © Jerry Pavia.

p. 342: Photo © Tim Street-Porter.

p. 343: (top left) Photo © Lee Anne White; Design: Joan Lewis & Nancy Caplan; (top right) Photo © Deidra Walpole; Design: Jeni Cunningham; (bottom) Photo © Tim Street-Porter; Design: Laura Dunas.

p. 344: (left) Photo by Jennifer Brown, © The Taunton Press, Inc.; (top right) Photo © Jerry Pavia; (bottom) Photo © Allan Mandell; Design: Steve Ansell & Collin Lichtensteiger.

p. 345: Photo © Jerry Pavia.

p. 346: (top) Photo © Alan & Linda Detrick; Design: Dinky Baylinson; (bottom) Photo © Dency Kane; Design: Don Morris & Harry White.

p. 347: (top) Photo © Dency Kane; Design: Don Morris & Harry White; (bottom) Photo © Alan & Linda Detrick; Design: Marilyn Coombe Stewart.

CHAPTER 10

p. 348: Todd Caverly, photographer © 2005, Brian Vanden Brink photos

p. 350: (top) Photo © Linda Svendsen; (bottom) Photo © Robert Perron

p. 351: (top) Photo © Brian Vanden Brink; (bottom) Photo by Andy Engel, © The Taunton Press, Inc.

p. 352: (top) Photo © Linda Svendsen; (bottom) Photo © Brian Vanden Brink

p. 353: (top) Photo © Brian Vanden Brink; (bottom) Photo © Chipper Hatter; (right) Photo © Linda Svendsen

p. 354: Photo © Brian Vanden Brink

p. 355: (top) Photo © Brian Vanden Brink; (right & bottom) Photos © Chipper Hatter

pp. 356-357: Photos © Lee Anne White

p. 358: (left & top right) Photos © Brian Vanden Brink; (bottom right) Photo © 2005 Carolyn L. Bates/www.carolynbates.com

p. 359: (top) Photo © Robert Perron; (bottom) Photo © Linda Svendsen

p. 360: Photo © Brian Vanden Brink

p. 361: (top) Photo © Chipper Hatter; (bottom) Photo by Roe A. Osborn, © The Taunton Press, Inc.

p. 362: (top) Photo © Robert Perron; (bottom left) Photo © Brian Vanden Brink; (bottom right) Photo © 2005 Carolyn L. Bates/www.carolynbates.com

p. 363: Photo © Lee Anne White

p. 364: (top) Photo © Robert Perron; (bottom) Photo © Brian Vanden Brink

p. 365: (top left) Photo © 2005 Carolyn L. Bates/www.carolynbates.com; (top right) Photo © Linda Svendsen; (bottom) Photo © Robert Perron

p. 366: Photo © Ken Gutmaker

p. 367: (top left & bottom) Photos © Lee Anne White; (top right) Photo © Rob Karosis

p. 368: (top) Photo © www.davidduncanlivingston.com; (bottom) Photo © Robert Perron

p. 369: Photo © Brian Vanden Brink

p. 370: (top) Photo © Mary Rezny; Architect: Brent Richards, Ross/Tarrant Architects, Inc., Lexington, KY; (bottom left) Photo by Andy Engel, © The Taunton Press, Inc.; Builder: Ken Troupe, Sudbury, ON; (bottom right) Photo by Andy Engel, © The Taunton Press, Inc.

p. 371: (top) Photo by Charles Miller, © The Taunton Press, Inc.; (bottom left) Photo courtesy Plow and Hearth; (bottom right) Photo by John Rickard, © The Taunton Press, Inc.

p. 372: (top) Photo © Robert Perron; (bottom) Photo © Ken Gutmaker

p. 373: (top left) Photo by William Kaufman, © The Taunton Press, Inc.; (top right) Photo © Ken Gutmaker; WESKETCH Architects; (bottom) Photo © LindaSvendsen